COLORADO
AVALANCHE
DISASTERS

✦ *An Untold Story of the Old West* ✦

BY JOHN W. JENKINS

WESTERN REFLECTIONS
PUBLISHING COMPANY
Ouray, Colorado

2001
First Edition
Printed in the United States of America

ISBN 1-890437-44-1
Library of Congress Catalog Number 99-67793
Cover and book design by Laurie Goralka Design

Western Reflections Publishing Company
P.O. Box 710
Ouray, CO 81427

*Dedicated to Shirley and Harvey Doidge,
and the pioneers who risked all to settle
and build Colorado. A special dedication
to Deborah T. Jenkins for unwavering
support and assistance in the production
of this book.*

Unknown location of avalanche closing a railroad in Colorado. As the track is standard gauge it may be in Glenwood Canyon on the Denver and Rio Grande or along the Colorado Midland. (Colorado Historical Society)

TABLE OF CONTENTS

Avalanche snow tunnel on the Million Dollar Highway — Red Mountain Pass. This tunnel lasted until spring when warming temperatures softened the rock-hard avalanche enough for men with picks and shovels to clear the road. (Grant Houston Collection, Lake City)

INTRODUCTION

Colorado Avalanche Disasters:
An Untold Story of the Old West

> *" . . . The snow cloud was vast with the sun lighting up the glinting particles near the fringe of the swirling mass. The center was like a giant waterfall, while the turbulent clouds spread out on either side as if wanting to start their own streams. The swirling snow was creating ever-changing ring patterns illuminated by the sun. The ground shook as in an earthquake, and the noise as the snow crashed down over the rocks into the valley was overwhelming."* — Colin Fraser, *Avalanche and Snow Safety.*[1]

Before starting a history of Colorado avalanche disasters, a discussion of avalanche formation and some history of avalanche disasters throughout the world is necessary.

People recognize the word "avalanche" everywhere in the world as meaning an irresistible, overpowering, and totally destructive force, which leaves no sense of hope for anyone caught in its unrelenting power. The slide described in the opening quote occurred on March 6, 1898. It fulfilled every expectation of a powerful avalanche. It descended over 5000 vertical feet in a run extending over four and a third miles. The slide crossed the valley floor a distance of one and a half miles and ran thousands of feet up the opposite side — its plume of snow blotting out the sun. The slide's speed was estimated at 225 miles per hour or three and three-quarter miles per minute. It is easy to see that skiing out of an avalanche to safety is unlikely. This book examines the human perceptions of avalanches in an historical perspective, but long before settlers came to Colorado people living in the Alps of Europe had already experienced centuries of avalanche disasters.

In the Alps, avalanches have had a great impact on humans. So common is this threat that the phenomenon is known as the Avalanche Beast. Through the centuries hundreds have died from Das Lautier — the avalanche beast. Modern technology has slowed, but not eradicated the threat. As recently as the winter of 1999, dozens died at resorts in Switzerland during one of the heaviest snow years on record. The beast has shown its force many times throughout history. From ancient times through the Middle Ages to the present, avalanches have frightened and intrigued traveler and villager. Poet Silius Italicus (b. 25 A.D.) wrote an account of a seriously destructive avalanche in the Alps when Rome was expanding its empire in the third century B.C. Rome's primary rival lay threatening across the sea in North Africa. During the Punic War in 218 B.C., the brilliant Carthaginian general Hannibal determined to stop Rome's ambitions by an invasion of the Latin Peninsula. After conquering the Iberian Peninsula, Hannibal brought an army of nearly 40,000 men, 8,000 horses, and dozens of elephants over the Alps. Nearly half the men, a quarter of the horses, and several elephants were killed by exposure to cold, snow and avalanches. Hannibal watched as one avalanche swept hundreds of men and dozens of animals away, burying them from sight.

Hannibal's problem with avalanches is only one of the first on record. Many times armies suffered casualties from the White Death in the Alps. In 1478 the Dukes of Uri and Milan were engaged in a war. The Zurchers, allied with Milan, rushed an army over the Alps at St. Gotthard Pass. An avalanche suddenly swept away sixty of the mercenary soldiers. At the close of that century, France's Louis XI and the Prince of Milan fought the Swabian War. Thousands of soldiers crossed and re-crossed the mountains through Switzerland at the Great St. Bernard Pass. One avalanche killed 100 men and dozens more died in other incidents. At nearly the same time Kaiser Maximilian crossed with 10,000 soldiers at Ofen Pass where an avalanche buried 400 men. Remarkably all were found alive.

Pilgrimages created heavy traffic over the Alps during the Middle Ages as thousands crossed the Alps from continental Europe en route to Rome or the Holy Land. Rudolf, the Abbot of St. Trond, crossed the Great St. Bernard in December 1128 and noted the distresses of a winter crossing. Heavy snow and drifting stranded thousands of pilgrims at Saint Rhemy. Anxious to continue their journey the pilgrims bribed local guides, called marones, to strike a path and take them through. Leaving the pilgrims praying in the village church the marones trekked out of town when

> *. . . an enormous mass of snow like a mountain slipped from the rocks and carried them away, as it seemed to the depths of hell. Those who had been aware of the avalanche . . . made a hasty and furious dash to the murderous spot and having dug out the marones carried them back some . . . quite lifeless, others half dead . . . and dragging others with broken limbs."* [2]

This incident convinced the pilgrims that entrance to the Kingdom could wait. They quickly retreated to the safety of shelters until the snow fury ended.

During the Middle Ages avalanches took their toll on villages and farms with increasing regularity. A population explosion in the fourteenth century followed the years of the Black Death as better sanitation and improved food supplies extended life expectancy. Villages grew beyond old limits and new ones appeared higher in valleys. Exposure increased. Record keeping also improved with the mass production of paper and introduction of the printing press in the fifteenth century. Records of deaths and their causes were documented in newspaper accounts and official documents. Such sources often document the loss of entire villages. In an instant, several generations of families could be swept into eternity. Some locations were hit several times. Homes and villages were often rebuilt in areas proven dangerous only to be destroyed again and again with loss of life. People also created the condition of danger. Protective forest cover was stripped away to build houses destabilizing the slopes. Avalanches descended destroying the houses built from trees that had originally held the snow in place.

Leukarbad is a case in point. This town is known for its healing hot water mineral baths and has been hit several times over three centuries with dozens of people killed. The town was always rebuilt in the same place. A slide in 1518 took sixty-one lives. Two hundred years later fifty-five died. In an avalanche survival tale one man, Stephen Roten, survived eight days trapped in a wine cellar. Again in 1720 and 1758 avalanches spread across the baths and homes of Leukerbad.[3] Each time the town was rebuilt, and it exists today under the same threat.

Napoleon's wars in 1799 and 1800 brought the great armies of Austria and Russia to fight France in the Alps. Russian General Suvarow defeated the French in a battle on St. Gotthard Pass. The French were forced to retreat to the Lake of Four Cantons. Suvarow was unable to follow the French in their retreat and finish off the victory. Instead, he led his army across several passes to cut off the French. On Panixer Pass heavy snowfall created the kind of avalanche conditions that run with very little triggering. Hundreds of men and animals died.

On the way to the Battle of Marengo in November 1899 Napoleon guided his army over the Alps. He instructed General Lannes to order soldiers not to " . . . cry or call out for fear of causing a fall of avalanches."[4] Heavy artillery cradled in hollowed-out tree trunks were dragged over the passes. These set off several avalanches and buried dozens of men. Another general of Napoleon, Marechel MacDonald, watched as " . . . many men were entombed . . . ."[5] One of MacDonald's officers wrote later of his horror while he watched avalanches claim so many of his men:

An enormous avalanche loosing itself from the highest summit, rolling with a fearful noise and gliding with the rapidity of lightning, carried off 30 dragoons at the head of the column who, with their horses, were swept away by the torrent, dashed against the rocks and buried under the snow. I was not 150 paces from the spot and thought for the moment that General Laboissiere and his officers had likewise been swept away.[6]

The men, demoralized and fearful, refused to cross until MacDonald himself rallied the men and led them through the storming and avalanching pass.

World War I broke all records for death during a war, including avalanche fatalities. In December 1916, one of the worst storms on record created avalanches that wiped out entire barracks and killed hundreds. Slides caught patrols or battalions in movement. Avalanches were made into a weapon of war. Both sides fired artillery shells above each other's positions. As many as 3,000 Austrians, and maybe that number of Italians, died in a forty-eight hour period from this ugly business of mass murder. Some were rescued, but most died of injuries and suffocation. Many lie buried to this day.[7] Estimates range between 40,000 to 80,000 avalanche fatalities in the Alps during World War I. Destruction to armies by avalanches is not lost in history. In 1973 the Chinese army lost a thousand troops in Tibet to the White Death.

Many myths about avalanches have come down through the centuries. Sometimes discerning myth from truth is difficult. Before scientists really studied avalanche formation people believed an avalanche started as a snowball. As the ball rolled downhill it gathered more snow until it became a monster capable of wiping out entire towns. Research long ago disproved the snowball theory. Another myth is that loud noises such as gunshots or sonic booms set off a slide. No known studies support this theory. Another belief is that trees always stabilize snowpack and prevent avalanches from starting. Trees or boulders have been shown to offer some stability to snowpack, but with certain snow conditions, trees and boulders will not stop an avalanche from running.

The conditions leading to avalanche danger are varied and depend on climate and terrain. Most mountainous regions of the world are along coastlines. The major exceptions are the Himalayas, the Urals in Russia and the Rocky Mountains. The Alps, while somewhat inland, are close to the Mediterranean and have a more marine type of climate. Location is important as it affects the type of snowfall, amounts, and weather conditions. Along coastlines the climate is marine. Moisture from oceans feeds heavy snowfall. Avalanche danger increases soon after a storm begins and lasts for a few hours or days after it ends. A marine climate is warmer than a continental climate. Snowpack tends to stabilize throughout its depth since there is little difference between temperatures at the snow surface and those at the ground.

Mountain ranges far from a coast have what is known as a continental weather system. Snowfall is generally less but the climate is colder. Avalanche danger increases with heavy snowfall during the storm and continues high for hours or days as it does in a marine climate. What makes a continental mountain climate more dangerous is the formation of temperature gradient layers. After a storm passes, air temperature drops to low levels. Snow insulates the ground keeping temperatures warmer there than at the surface. The warmer snow at ground level melts, refreezes, and over time metamorphoses into unconsolidated ice crystals. These ice crystals are like ball bearings, having no cohesion, and are unable to support the pack above under certain conditions — as when a skier adds more weight. This special continental condition creates avalanche danger throughout the entire winter season long after storms have passed.

This explanation is only part of the story. Avalanche danger forms for other reasons and is complicated and difficult to accurately predict. Heavy snowfall over a short period of time dramatically increases danger. After a storm passes falling temperatures tend to maintain danger since snow remains unconsolidated. Often this new snow covers crusty and icy older pack that has formed through a process of thawing and refreezing. Sudden warming or spring temperatures loosen snowpack and cause natural sliding. These conditions are faced in the Colorado Rockies all winter, but it is temperature gradient for- mation that creates the most danger and is hardest to assess since it is unseen. Temperature gradient layers may exist from early winter into spring and not give the slightest indication that a slide might happen. At any time an event can cause a change in equilibrium and start an avalanche. Animals crossing a weak slope, a person on skis or riding a snowmobile, or high winds can start snow sliding, catching all in its way and sometimes descending on camp or town. Almost always the avalanche that kills is the one set off by the person killed. The Rockies have these conditions, and Colorado has more avalanche accidents and fatalities then any other state for this reason.

Another myth applies to the technique for crossing dangerous slopes. Knowledgeable people use extra caution when crossing a sus- pected slope. Skiers suspecting danger prudently stop and plan a safe crossing. The first person in the party goes across while others wait and watch carefully to see where the person ends up if a slide occurs; but after one or two others cross, the remaining party may throw caution to the wind and start across. The slope fractures and all are carried away. One person crossing at a time is safest and there are fewer risks. That one person or a dozen have crossed a suspected slope does not mean the slope is stable. It can run at any time under the lightest loading.

A truth about avalanches is that survival rate is low. Researchers estimate that there is only a ten percent chance of survival after the first half-hour of being buried alive. No person buried more than seven feet has ever survived, unless there were some extraneous circum- stances such as an air pocket formed by debris. The best chance for survival is by the victim's companions performing a prompt rescue. Of all the truths about avalanches, a most terrifying actuality is that victims often hear rescuers above, but only rarely do rescuers hear cries for help from below.

Scientists have accumulated data and classified avalanches into types. Powder avalanches tend to take to the air in a billowing cloud. These are most survivable but still can kill. A loose snow avalanche starts at a single point and picks up more volume as it moves. A slab avalanche starts by the formation of a long crack at the starting point and then moves in mass. Slab avalanches may have hard blocks of snow as large as small trucks or just be loose snow. Slab avalanches are the most dangerous. The surface on which sliding takes place can be along the ground, sometimes called a "climax," at a shear layer within the snowpack or where temperature gradient layers exist. Avalanches can be dry and powdery, wet and heavy, or form hard blocks. Both wet and dry avalanches can flow along the surface, fly up into the air, or do both while in motion. The track of an avalanche follows terrain features termed confined or unconfined. Unconfined avalanches occur in large open areas such as basins above timberline, but may also be on any hillside, or in trees, where a gully does not cut the hill. Where a gully does cut down a slope the avalanche may follow it, becoming "channeled." While all avalanches are potentially deadly, a channeled avalanche squeezes more mass into a confined space making for deeper burial and less certain survival.[8]

Some people caught in an avalanche die of injuries soon after the catastrophe begins as the body is pulled in many directions from the turbulent flow of the slide. Many survive after the ride ends, and as the snow settles, it packs the person so tightly that not even a finger can be moved. In a few minutes the end usually comes through asphyxiation as the panicked victim consumes the small amount of air available. Only a few survive the ordeal if not found within a few minutes, although a few have lived for hours or even days.

Many factors can contribute to living — the severity of injury, availability of oxygen, and most importantly the condition of the person and mental strength. Rescuers know that debris or large blocks of snow can grind and tear a person to death. The victim is smashed against trees or boulders and may be killed, but the leading cause of death is suffocation in the few minutes after the avalanche settles. If the victim survives the initial slide then personal physical and emotional condition may be the deciding factor in how long a victim survives. Even a few extra minutes can mean the difference between being found alive or dead. Survival is more likely if the victim is trapped in the first three feet from the surface, and if an air pocket is formed allowing some breathing time. In one case of survival a stream in the gulch below the buried victim melted the snow away in time to deliver lifesaving oxygen. Others have been trapped and left for dead for several hours, days, or even weeks and still lived. In other cases an avalanche captured a victim in a building, but a beam lodged in such a way that an air pocket was created and provided protection against crushing.

Even if the victim is fortunate enough to have his head or a limb exposed above the surface he may find himself helpless and unable to dig out. If limbs are buried, movement can be completely restricted. Rescuers can tell that a person survived the run of the avalanche by an ice mask. Snow melts around the face and then refreezes creating a mask. The start, the ride, and the ending are all a nightmare. A sense of powerlessness reigns over the avalanche victim in the midst of an overwhelming force.

Every year hundreds of people lose their lives in avalanches throughout the world. In recent years most are engaged in recreation, usually in some form of mountaineering activity. In the Alps, where serious mountaineering first developed, climbers and later skiers, became increasingly those most at risk. The first recorded death in the Alps of a recreation related accident was on Mount Blanc on August 20, 1820.[9]

In the western hemisphere avalanches have taken a deadly toll, but not to the extent experienced in more populated Europe. The North American continent with it's more sparse population has experienced tragedy in smaller numbers. Yet individuals faced suffering from the very beginning of exploration and settlement. When the mountain ranges of the West revealed valuable resources, the influx of prospectors, settlers, and later railroads, exposed them to the danger of heavy snows and resulting avalanche. People in camps and towns and at mining sites faced the danger throughout winter and in some areas all year long. Toward the end of the nineteenth century mining declined, and exposure to danger subsided. Then in 1910 the greatest avalanche tragedy in the United States took place. In March, three trains stood snowbound near Wellington in Washington State's Cascade Mountains near Stevens Pass. A single avalanche brushed the trains off the track and into the valley below. Nearly a hundred died. This disaster inspired the building of a tunnel to remove this danger to travelers through the Cascades[10]

Twentieth century progress and technology have actually increased exposure to snowslides. Private transportation gives greater numbers of people easy access to remote areas. Improvements in transportation, more time for recreation, and increased popularity of Nordic and Alpine skiing and travel by snowmobile bring more visitors into avalanche country. Interestingly the total number of those killed in avalanches has not increased in proportion. Several factors can explain this. At Alta, Utah, in 1937 the Forest Service set up the first avalanche research station in the western hemisphere for the purpose of studying conditions preceding avalanching.[11] Alta is an appropriate place for this station since some of the deadliest of the nation's slide disasters occurred here. In 1874 an avalanche descended on this mining community and killed sixty men, women, and children.[12] In 1884 another slide killed twelve, and in 1885, sixteen perished.[13] The Alta center and others such as the Colorado Avalanche Information Center continue to improve forecasting of avalanche danger. Communication has improved over the years to warn people of the perils of mountaineering. Efforts by local, state and federal agencies, search and rescue groups, and mountaineering-related business have increased public knowledge. Their efforts have been a major factor in fewer numbers of victims than were caught in disasters in the nineteenth century. Trained ski patrol groups make ski areas safer using avalanche control techniques. The media helps by reporting warnings of danger and predicting weather conditions. Improvement in construction of highways and protective structures such as snow fences and snowsheds over highways decrease the danger to highway travelers. Most of all, awareness enables the mountaineer and skier to take a moment for sober and intelligent thought wherever adventure may lead.

CHAPTER 1

Shining Mountains, Gilded Streams and White Death: Avalanches in Early Colorado History

> *"The street was very quiet. There were no wagons, no horses; only footsteps on the board sidewalks, or the bark of a dog. I heard a distant rumble that sounded like thunder in the mountains; it grew heavier, the walk under my feet shook, and then, with a loud roar, the sound stopped. I wondered if it could be an earthquake; no one on the walk seemed to notice it so I asked a passing miner what that noise was.*
>
> *"Why, man alive," he exclaimed, "don't you know snowslides when you hear them?"* — Charles Fox Gardiner, *Doctor at Timberline.* [14]

Located in the middle of the North American Continent, Colorado has the highest average altitude of any state including Alaska. Throughout Colorado's history the mountains have been the focus of the area's economic development and the main attraction for people who come from all over the world to visit or live here. Many come to see the beauty of mountains and climb hundreds of peaks that rise from wide broad valleys called parks. Others descend great canyons in rafts and kayaks near the headwaters of many of the West's greatest rivers, the Arkansas, Colorado, Rio Grande, and North and South Platte. Millions visit each year to ski and snowboard at world-class ski areas. Others take to the backcountry on skis, snowshoes and snowmobiles deep into Colorado's numerous mountain ranges, many of which reach high above timberline, some over 14,000 feet in altitude. While the search for precious metals first brought large numbers to settle, it is recreation that has dominated Colorado's mountain economy since after World War II. Throughout Colorado history, avalanches have taken a toll on those who venture into the mountains. Much scientific study has been given to the avalanche phenomena in recent years although the problem has existed for Coloradoans since the first gold strikes in the mid-nineteenth century. Every avalanche fatality is a family and personal disaster, but present total numbers are few compared to the tally during the heyday of mining and mountain railroading. In at least one year over fifty deaths were counted.

During the nineteenth century avalanches destroyed property and injured or killed hundreds of people in Colorado, mostly those associated with mining. Today a few avalanche fatalities occur each year. Avalanches in the Colorado Rockies cause more property damage, injury and death, than in any other state in the country, including Alaska, and fully one-third more than second place Washington State.[15]

In mountain valleys and on slopes of alpine peaks prospectors searched for wealth, or they lived at exposed sites while they removed the valuable ores. During the height of mining, people traveled from point to point through dangerous territory, and mail carriers took mail over high, avalanche prone mountain passes. In the mountains, life proceeded as usual throughout the winter, broken occasionally by a sharp crack, or a sound like distant thunder, as cornices or deep snowpack broke and ran headlong into valleys below. Usually, no damage resulted as slides generally ran their courses in remote areas. From time to time, a slide would break its usual boundaries and descend, rolling, boiling relentlessly, gaining velocity and mass along the way. Encountering the works of men it tore away all in its path, leaving flat the hopes and aspirations of labor and investment and sometimes taking life. Accounts tell of miners sitting securely in their cabins who died, not from crushing tonnage, but from suffocation as the slide passed over, sucking life-sustaining air from the unwary victims inside. Some were struck and buried for long periods and survived unscathed, while some suffocated under a few inches of snow. The stories of these disasters present tales of great suffering, and sometimes triumph over peril. The danger of an avalanche is always a constant, deadly, and destructive possibility in Colorado's high country. Slides can occur anywhere, and unexpectedly, even in places not being prone to avalanches. In Colorado avalanches have run in every month of the year. As presented in the following pages, slides have cost hundreds of lives and destroyed millions of dollars in property in Colorado. More than 500 people have perished in avalanches during Colorado's history. The danger is present in every season wherever there are mountains and snowfall.

People coming west faced many perils in stride, even when encountering devastation from the great winter danger of high mountain regions — the avalanche. From the earliest days of exploration by the Spanish, through the trapping and mining eras, pioneering and settlement, winter snows affected Colorado's development. Individuals were drawn to the Colorado Rockies for a variety of reasons. Some came for the adventure of settling a wilderness and tapping its great resources. Others came to improve their health in a dry climate. Many came to invest fortunes in mining and railroads or simply to enjoy the beautiful backbone of the continent. Few were deterred by common threats like quickly rising rivers during spring snowmelt, bitter cold, deep winter snows, or avalanches.

Even the warming spring brought White Death's final assault. Snow holding fast throughout the winter lost its grip on high peaks and descended headlong to valley floors. Spring renewed the lush vegetation and water cascaded down steep gulches fed by receding snowfields. The warm temperatures ended winter's siege. Towns and camps " . . . would be alive with a general jubilation when the tinkling bells of the first train of jacks was heard in the spring, for that meant the end of a six month's siege in the midst of impassable snow."[16]

Sparse population kept exposure to avalanches in Colorado low before the Gold Rush of 1859. During that year an estimated 100,000 people stampeded to the new gold fields. From then on prospectors, miners, mail carriers, railroad workers, and travelers entered the mountains and were exposed to deadly avalanches. Prospectors found outcroppings on high peaks where the weathering stripped away surface rock revealing ore lying underneath. Avalanches aided this weathering, carrying away overburden and exposing rich ore outcroppings. Miners traveled, worked, and lived in avalanche-prone areas, and intense mining placed Colorado's population centers in the mountains for decades. Camps and towns sprang up close to mines. Pioneers knew avalanche possibilities existed, but no one could predict when they would occur. Mining companies took some, but usually inadequate, precautions. The only real defense was luck, and that occasionally ran out.

These miners skied or snowshoed to the mine for a day's work but first had to clear away an avalanche from the portal. (Denver Public Library, Western History Department)

Colorado's most famous silver tycoon, Horace Tabor, lost a claim to simple rumors of avalanches. In 1859 Tabor left Golden City with wife Augusta and son Maxie to look for gold in the mountains west of town. They met a prospector who warned of terrible avalanche dangers in the winter. Augusta became alarmed and insisted on returning to Golden City during this season. While they were gone, the prospector jumped Tabor's claim.[17]

The prospector, not altogether untruthful in his warning, relied upon knowledge that avalanches along the Front Range on the eastern edge of the Rockies in Colorado had already claimed lives. In fact one of the earliest recorded fatalities in Colorado territory is reported in the *Rocky Mountain News* story, "Man Lost in an Avalanche." C. M. Ferrell of Golden City was near the North Fork of the South Platte and witnessed it. Ferrell said that while he was prospecting, he saw two men carried by a great snowslide into " . . . a steep declivity, nearly a thousand feet." J. T. Shelter and his brother became victims of an " . . . immense slide with trees, rocks, and loose earth." J. T. Shelter's brother was found and saved.[18]

Later, in 1862, the *Colorado Republican* reported "An Immense Snowslide" that swept down a mountain above Washington Gulch on January 20 and

> *. . . accelerating in velocity as it progressed down, . . . and carrying along whole forests of giant-pines as they stood in its track . . . swept all before it until reaching . . . the main gulch . . . shaving off the tops of the trees that stood in the gulches below. After reaching the base of the mountain, its wild career continued for over a mile, when coming to the main gulch it tumbled its exhausted fury in one conglomerate mass into the canon. A collection of some dozen cabins which lay in the direction of its spent career were entirely covered to a depth of above ten feet in the mass of snow and debris, but fortunately none were hurt.*[19]

The same *Republican* issue reported John Aldrich's death in Washington Gulch. Aldrich with several companions was traveling from Washington Gulch to Denver. Luck originally seemed to be with him since he had departed before the big slide in the gulch, but while crossing Cochetopa Pass an avalanche caught him and his friends. Everyone except Aldrich managed to dig out. His companions searched an hour and a half before discovering his body under eight feet of snow.[20]

One spring, Frank Brown, the manager of the Farwell properties near Independence Pass, traveled to inspect the mines. Looking for a place to camp for the night, he came across a body exposed in avalanche debris. Frank recognized the man as one who had been seen before at Independence while prospecting in Lost Man Gulch on the Roaring Fork River. At least once during the preceding year he had sold high-grade ore at Leadville. He had not been noticed in Leadville, or anywhere else for a time, until Brown saw his body. The miner never revealed his mine's location, but many remembered the ore's extremely high quality and looked for the claim. They never found it, although the nearby camps of Ruby and Lincoln Gulch eventually yielded a respectable amount of gold and may be part of the vein the dead miner discovered in Lost Man Gulch.[21]

Pioneers knew Sts. John (named for the two Saint Johns) in Summit County near Breckenridge as a place of deep snows and avalanches. Residents often heard huge slides coming down after every snowstorm. Sometimes an avalanche reached the edge of a camp or miner's cabin without damage. After one such slide, a miner dug out, and needing firewood, cut a nearby tree poking up from the debris. In the spring, he discovered the stump to be twelve feet high.[22] Boston Silver Mining Company took control of Sts. John in 1878. It became a company town with the best facilities provided for miners and the latest in milling and smelting techniques.[23] Throughout the "winter of the big snow" of 1899, avalanches descended to the very edge of Sts. John. Snow piled so deeply that people entered and exited buildings only through second-story windows.[24]

In the late 1860s General Buford discovered the Victoria Mine near the town of Frisco. Located on Royal Mountain the Victoria Mine was at the terminus of a great avalanche run. A few years later investors from Masontown, Pennsylvania bought the Victoria Mine, and the few buildings composing this settlement were re-christened Masontown. One winter evening in 1912 an avalanche ran over Masontown. It harmed no one since everyone had gone down the valley to a party at Frisco.[25]

Avalanche disasters came early to the Front Range. Prospectors fanned out into the hills west of Denver City finding placers and silver lodes. Surface ores were quickly claimed and soon mined out leaving only subsurface lodes. Silver in its hard rock matrix resisted the heat of smelting, vaporizing into the air rather than consolidating into silver globules. Mining declined in Colorado almost to the point of extinction. When a way was found to separate silver from its ore, mining in the areas around Georgetown, Silver Plume, Geneva, and Montezuma revived.

Miner Charles Fix left Montezuma in February 1874 for quail hunting. After he failed to return, his brother became alarmed and went searching. Following tracks he came upon a large avalanche where his brother's footprints entered but did not leave. A search party spent days looking for the body but to no avail.[26]

On Democrat Mountain near Georgetown, Charles Ritchie was carried over a precipice and killed on February 15, 1874. In April 1875 at the Champion lode in Geneva District six miners ate breakfast in their cabin. Suddenly a low rumble was heard and before the men could react they found themselves buried beneath the wreckage of their cabin under tons of snow. All survived unharmed except for one man who was slightly injured. The men rebuilt the cabin and an avalanche never came that way again.[27] On February 13, 1879 the Geneva district experienced another slide that caught Nicholas Benny and Dan Cameron. Benny perished, but although badly injured, Cameron survived. On the same day two men leading a team of burros in Geneva district at Smoky Hollow were carried away in a massive slide. Both men survived but all the burros died.[28] Just four days later in the same district eleven men were swept away. All survived except Charles Allen. Then in 1881 in a gulch between Brown and Hanna Mountains an avalanche struck the cabin occupied by Jim, William, and Knox Pinckard and the cook named Lucy Jones. Lucy and Knox were killed, but William was rescued alive. Some suspected that when Jim Pinckard left camp, his yelling "good-bye" started the slide.

Spring is well under way but this huge avalanche has yet to yield to being cleared from Red Mountain Pass. Notice the hillsides no longer have snow. (Grant Houston Collection, Lake City)

In late March 1875 miners in a cabin heard the sound of a huge slide coming down from a mountain. They quickly ran out and barely avoided death from the collapsing roof. One man, James O'Fallon, embraced a huge pine tree as the snow rushed past. In nearby Georgetown, people could hear the sound of the slide. Alarm bells rang. Several hundred men threaded their way up the mountain with picks, shovels, and explosives. They came upon the slide in a gulch near Silver Creek. The deep gorge was filled with green trees, huge boulders, and a mass of snow. Rescuers saw a huge fracture line high above them where the slide had started near the peak's summit at the head of the gulch. They found James O'Fallon partially buried, but he was unable to extricate himself. Transported to town by wagon, O'Fallon gave his account of the harrowing drama to the *Georgetown Miner* which was reported by the *Greeley Tribune* newspaper.

> *. . . He and his brother had been working on a lode in that vicinity and occupied a cabin situated on a side of a gulch. The brother and Jasper Bell had gone up on the hill some little time before the accident, leaving James in the cabin. He [James] heard roaring noises and stepped out of the cabin, only to see the rushing avalanche of boulders and snow coming down the gulch. He jumped behind a pine tree for protection, but a moment afterwards the tree is torn out by the roots and James is carried down the gulch with the tree lying across his breast. Fortunately, an immense rock struck the tree with such force as to hurl it off his body, but he was unable to extricate himself from the avalanche and was carried about 400 feet . . .*[29]

A few days later James O'Fallon succumbed to his injuries.[30]

In another incident W. G. Morgan, Chris Jensen, and Patterson Martin came up missing. Attempts to reach and find their cabin failed. Not until late April 1875 were the frozen bodies found. Searchers speculated the avalanche had buried the men for several weeks.

> *. . . The slide had evidently swept off the roof, which was carried some little distance away, without disturbing the walls. The snow had then filled the house, was packed in hard and frozen. Those who were digging soon uncovered a man's hand. Martin and Jensen were found lying in a natural position, in bed, as though they had died without waking from their sleep. Morgan's body was partly out and partly in bed; he had probably awakened, and was about to arise when the falling snow enveloped him.*[31]

Nearly two years later in 1877, across the range in South Park an avalanche tragedy took place near Whale Peak. The Whale Mine sat at the head of Hall's Gulch. Hall's Gulch joined the South Platte River at Webster at the eastern base of Kenosha Pass. The Whale Mine produced from 1869 into the 1870s. The Denver, South Park and Pacific Railroad built a spur to the mill and smelter. Its rich silver barite ore supported a town of three hundred. The mine owners constructed a bunkhouse one thousand feet above the valley floor, and eight hundred feet below the summit. They allowed for the possibility of an avalanche by placing the bunkhouse under rocky ledges. It was hoped these measures would stop or deflect an avalanche. The growth of large trees above and below the ledges indicated slides never passed that way.

At 10:00 a.m. on a cold morning of January 7, 1877, after a period of heavy snowfall combined with blowing and drifting, an avalanche started at the head of Hall Valley. It reached the bunkhouse and its inhabitants without warning, sweeping all far into Hall Gulch. An early pioneer doctor, Charles Gardiner, described

> *. . . a huge slide rushed down the gulch back of the house and across the valley floor, taking the big log bunkhouse with it as if it consisted of cards, crushing the big logs like straw, burying it at last under tons of ice and snow. I saw the place with the scattered and splintered logs, pieces of bedding and clothes, all tumbled around and crushed among the rocks where the poor fellows met their death. . . .*[32]

The slide hit and removed the bunkhouse a quarter mile down Hall's Gulch, killing five unwary inhabitants. Owing to a break in the telegraph lines between Morrison and Hall's Gulch word of the disaster did not reach Denver for nine days. J. McDonald relayed the information from Grant that five people had died. When it occurred, all the inhabitants of the boardinghouse were sitting around the stove, as all were found close to it and near each other.

A search party quickly formed to find if there was any life among the avalanche debris that covered a huge area. After digging and probing for days, they abandoned hope of a live rescue. The tightly-packed and debris-filled snow hid the bodies until spring. The dead were James Reed, his wife, and their boy along with John Reed and a man named Alfred.[33]

Another report in the same issue of the *Greeley Tribune* reported an avalanche at the Champion Lode at the head of the Snake River on January 8. Superintendent G. W. Lindgreen said that he and three others — Moses Profitt, J. Ruebard, and the cook French Pete — were in one of the houses at the mine when the slide struck at midnight. The building was about 1000 feet from the river and 800 feet below the summit. It was thought that cliffs overhead would protect the buildings. Flying over the cliffs the avalanche struck and took away the corner of the building filling the remaining portion with snow. French Pete was crushed and died instantly. Profitt and Ruebard were slightly covered and dug out unharmed. The survivors called for the superintendent and heard his voice a half-mile away. Locating the site where the voice emanated, the men dug him out from four feet of snow after three-quarters of an hour. Lindgreen reported that he managed to move his arm and clear snow away for breathing room, but as soon as he did more fell in and filled the space. The more he tried to clear the snow the more flowed in. He almost gave up hope when he heard the voices of his companions calling. With renewed hope he struggled to keep an airway open until he was freed. The snow in the Snake Valley was so deep and in danger of sliding that French Pete's body was left until safer conditions allowed for his removal for burial.[34]

Ready to push off on long skis. Skis could be up to eighteen feet in length. The pole acted as a rudder for turning. (Denver Public Library, Western History Department)

Miners, mail carriers, travelers, and railroads were exposed to avalanche danger much of the year. In southern Colorado the San Juan basin produced early destruction and loss of life.

Near and around Lake City steep mountains, plentiful snowfall, and narrow gulches produced dangerous avalanche conditions. The peaks above Lake City leave a lasting impression on anyone coming into this deep valley, remotely located between Gunnison and Creede. Gazing from ridges or low hills around Lake City, one can easily see some of Colorado's most impressive 14,000-foot peaks including Uncompahgre, Wetterhorn, Sunshine, Red Cloud, and Handies. On these slopes and on those of other peaks, not as lofty but just as impressive, are numerous avalanche paths.

When the Utes relinquished the San Luis Valley in 1868, settlers and prospectors came to the valley in great numbers. The treaty brought the whites closer to the silvery San Juans. Many settlers took the next step and began inevitable incursions into Ute territory looking for gold and precious metals. At the area around Lake City prospectors arrived as early as 1869. They found some gold, but development languished without roads into the rugged region.[35] Chief Ouray, realizing the futility of fighting against the superior numbers and resources of the whites negotiated the Brunot Treaty in 1874. Its terms gave the Utes $100,000 in cash to give up mineral lands of the San Juans, but the hot springs at the head of Uncompahgre River remained under Ute ownership. The treaty legalized prospecting and settlement throughout the San Juan basin.[36]

In the summer of 1874 Enos Hotchkiss, in partnership with the "Pathfinder of the San Juan," Otto Mears, left Saguache to survey a possible road to newly discovered San Juan Mines. Above Lake San Cristobal, Hotchkiss pinpointed a valuable outcropping of ore near where Alferd Packer ate his companions during a stressful winter in the snowy San Juans in 1873-1874. Hotchkiss' outcropping set off a rush. Many towns and camps sprang into existence including Lake City, Capitol City, Henson, and Rose's Cabin.[37] Several avalanche fatalities befell settlers, but most of these adversities were not of the scale of other San Juan regions. Two exceptions stood out. The 1887 slide at Vermont Mine took three lives, and four decades later one at Empire Chief Mine seized four men.

Henson Creek and the gulches and creeks feeding into that stream created a naturally troublesome avalanche area. Mudslides also played a part in Lake City's natural history. Nearby Lake San Cristobal, the largest natural lake in Colorado, formed behind a dam from a huge mudslide in the thirteenth century.[38]

One of the earliest avalanche fatalities in this area happened on February 18, 1878. It tore away C. C. Curtice's cabin in Boulder Gulch, an offshoot from Henson Creek. The slide apparently started four or five miles above and struck Curtice without warning. Curtice died in a relaxed position while reading. He still clutched his book when the searchers found his body.[39]

While traveling to Lake City, Charlie Murray was caught along with his horse in a slide at the head of American Basin that carried them at railroad speed for 200 yards. As the slide headed into timber Murray surfaced, and seeing a tree branch, grabbed it and held on tight. The power of the avalanche pulled him away but soon another branch came within reach and this time he was able to hold on as the slide passed. Unfortunately, he was buried to his neck and unable to move.

His cries alarmed Robert Kelly of the Hidden Treasure Lode who spent a half hour of hard digging before freeing Murray.[40]

In 1879, in a nearby gulch, Jackson Gregory and Joe Lytle laid in enough supplies at their diggings to last for a month so trips to town in winter could be avoided. Such trips exposed them to numerous avalanche paths that ran regularly. They would pass the snowy season at the Chipmunk Lode, planning its development, and then attempt to obtain fresh supplies after the most dangerous part of the season had passed. In late December 29, 1879, on a trip to Rose's Cabin for supplies they started back for the mine accompanied by mail carrier Frank Silance. When they reached the gulch where the men had to ascend to their mine they invited Silance for a visit, but he declined, anxious to continue on to Lake City. He said good-bye and continued on his way and never saw the men again. Soon after they parted an avalanche buried Lytle and Gregory. Each had been toting a powder keg from Rose's Cabin to their claim on Dolly Varden Mountain when the avalanche fell. Silance heard the noise, but did not realize that it had fallen down on his friends. Gregory and Lytle's weight started the slide. Tons of snow were set into motion, carrying them two thousand feet down the gulch. Many men at the mines on hillsides around them heard the slide but gave this common sound little notice. Miners at the Copper Glance on Copper Hill actually saw the men ascending the gulch before the avalanche but thought the men had already reached their cabin when it ran. Certainly, no one suspected that their colleagues had been entombed.

The next day some of the miners at the Copper Glance saw no activity at the Chipmunk Lode but concluded the men must be at work in the mine. The following day they still could not see any activity and decided to investigate. When they reached the cabin it was clear the men had never arrived, and the avalanche was clearly visible across the trail where the men had last been seen. Word was sent to Charlie Schaefer at Rose's Cabin who sent back the word that Gregory and Lytle had left two days before on Sunday afternoon. Gregory's family lived at Capitol City so it was hoped the men went there for celebrating New Year's, but word came back that they had not been there either. This left only one possibility — that the men lay under the terrible avalanche filling the gulch below Dolly Varden Mountain. The alarm was given and men from every mine and camp and from Capitol City poured into the search area. The men probed and dug trenches until by Wednesday afternoon the body of Gregory was revealed beneath four feet of snow. Tunnels were driven into the mass from several locations until finally the body of Lytle was recovered the next day. Both men died of asphyxiation.

The bodies were taken to Capitol City where Reverend George M. Darley provided services. Then the bodies were removed to Lake City for burial.[41]

No story of Colorado folklore is more enduring than one of a gold treasure that was found and then lost. There is a tale of an avalanche with just such a legend. It happened near Red Cliff but began at Fulford. *The Denver Republican* referred to Fulford in 1892 as having an "'. . . evil genius about the place' and hints at the 'spirits of men who lie buried' at the base of grim old Slate Mountain . . ."⁴²

Red Cliff, the Eagle County seat until 1921, received notice in 1878 when two Leadville prospectors found iron-stained outcroppings on Battle Mountain similar to the rich ores found at Leadville. The Little Ollie find set off a rush. Hundreds of people came to the area in any way possible including sleds, skis and snowshoes. The Battle Mountain Mining District was quickly established in 1879. Furious mining went on during warmer months, but most people left the area in winter owing to the ever-present avalanche danger. Battle Mountain referred to the ridge above town where a battle had ensued between Utes and Arapahoes in 1849. Locals named the camp Red Cliff for the red quartzite cliffs seen in the area.

In 1879, a party from Illinois prospected near Red Cliff above Eagle River. The party tried their luck as they passed through the Rockies and here they found a few nuggets. Several men decided to stay and over the next weeks reportedly extracted $100,000 in gold. They safeguarded the treasure in a drift. Signs of approaching winter incited survival concerns among the miners. They chose "Buck" Rogers to cross over to the nearest camp, and secure winter supplies. With enough gold dust to cover the cost of supplies, Buck set out to find a camp and buy provisions. Storm after storm slowed Buck's advance. Seven days later he made it to a camp several miles away. Knowing his return to be impossible until the weather broke, Buck began a round of drinking that lasted until the money ran out six weeks later. Finally sober, and suddenly alarmed, Buck hastily returned to seek his companions' fate. At the site where a makeshift cabin once stood he saw only a scoured and smooth stratum of slate stripped by the passing of a mighty avalanche.⁴³ In the gully below, a debris-filled snowslide completely obscured any sign of human industry or habitation. Rogers looked for help, but rescuers never found the men or the lost treasure.⁴⁴ Buck departed the area, and his moment in history, except for a map he left behind. A miner found Buck's map and went to the area to find that

> *. . . The slide had changed the entire appearance of the country. But the miner was lucky enough to dig where he finally found a tunnel, fragments of tools, human bones and pieces of ore, all tossed and thrown together by the tremendous forces of the slide.*⁴⁵

The man staked the claim, and seeking a partner, told Arthur Fulford about it. Before a partnership solidified the man died in a saloon brawl.[46] Arthur Fulford owned a ranch on Brush Creek in the 1880s. He was town marshall of Red Cliff and ran the stage stop called Halfway House between Eagle and Red Cliff. Fulford went to the dead man's cabin and found papers describing the site. He set out looking for the lost treasure and made his way to Red Cliff and Brush Creek as described by the miner. Someone who last saw him said he was " . . . looking gaunt and feverish, muttering about getting back to town in a couple of days."[47]

Fulford may have been caught and killed in an avalanche on New York Mountain around New Year's Day 1892. For two weeks, fifty men searched for his body, but they never found him or the treasure.[48]

In the Mountain Queen district, up Cement Creek from Silverton, mining companies developed large mines from rich ore deposits.[49] The town of Animas Forks was laid out in 1877. At an altitude of 11,500 feet, Animas Forks was among the highest mining camps in the country. Nearly a thousand people arrived and constructed buildings with steep-pitched roofs from finished lumber. Trees above the town were cut to provide the milled lumber for buildings. The barren hills alarmed the mayor. He feared avalanches would descend upon the town unchecked. Eventually, Animas Forks had a post office, saloon, store, hotel and two mills. It lay on the route between Silverton and Lake City. Otto Mears improved the road from Animas Forks to Eureka and added it to his toll road system. Later he extended the Silverton Northern Railroad from Eureka over the earlier wagon road to Animas Forks. Snow was a problem from the start. A substantially constructed snowshed on the railroad grade ended in splinters by an avalanche soon after completion.[50] One storm lasted twenty-three days and left snow twenty-five feet deep on Main Street. Once a swath of slide debris just outside of town extended half a mile and was 250 feet deep in places. Teamsters drove wagons over its rock-hard surface. In spring, a tunnel formed along the creek bed large enough for teams pulling wagons.

Silverton never experienced a direct hit, but slides often ran to the edge of town and closed the Denver and Rio Grande Railroad in Animas Canyon. More than once trains were blocked for days or even weeks and the citizens of Silverton faced the possibility of starvation. In gulches around Baker's Park it was a different story than in Silverton. Every year there were recorded avalanche destruction and loss of life. On a bright Sunday in 1878 J. L. Briggs, a partner in the Aspen Lode in Arrastra Gulch, left the cabin to get his skis at the dump for a trip to Silverton. When only a few feet from his skis a slide started and he was swept 2000 feet down the mountain almost into the gulch. Another partner, returning from Silverton noticed the footprints upon arriving at the

Aspen Mine. Following the tracks, he soon discovered the avalanche with tracks going in but not leaving the other side. After he contacted the men at the cabin they all went out to find Briggs. Seeing an unusual object sticking out of the slide far below they made their way along the boundary until presented with an awful sight. Brigg's body was face down, his legs protruding out, but he seemed lifeless. Only a few minutes were required to extricate the body that was taken to Quartzville.[51]

The Highland Mary Mine in Cunningham Gulch produced for several years without the hint of avalanche danger. Near the end of February 12, 1879, a slide appeared striking the shaft house and crushing it to pieces. "Big Dave" Olson managed to open the trapdoor of the shaft and jumped in followed by six others. Two remained at the surface unable to reach the shaft in time and they were crushed by collapsing debris of the shaft house. When all had settled down, a party was quickly formed at the mill that was untouched by the slide to go to the disaster and look for survivors. Upon reaching the site the rescuers came upon a mass of snowpack about four feet deep shattered like a broken window but still clinging to the hill. Most of the party feared going across the snowfield, but Phil Uhl and Jno. Klussman, thinking only of the victims, never hesitated and started across to search for the lost miners. They proceeded just a short distance when the snow gave way hurling them three hundred feet over a precipice to their deaths. Stephen Toy and Giovanni Anselmo had died at the shaft house. Phil Uhl and Jno. Klussman were carried over the precipice and joined the other two men in eternity. "Big Dave" and the others trapped in the shaft managed to dig out and all survived.[52]

The La Plata Miner reported an "Appalling Accident" at the Ajax Mine on Sultan Mountain March 7, 1878. The men turned in after working the day shift. With dinner finished they went to the shaft house where bunks were located. At daybreak three men at a nearby cabin left for their workings and noticed a slide had passed there during the night. Fearing the worst they made a fast dash to the Ajax Mine and discovered the building smashed to pieces. Owner H. L. Rogers who lived nearby was immediately contacted and he headed to Silverton for assistance. A large party arrived and recovered the bodies of all four men. Apparently they had gathered around the fire before turning in as all were in work clothes still warm and soggy with melted snow, and the fireplace logs were still warm to the touch. This placed the time of the slide at early night about eight or nine o'clock. The four deceased were James Jewell, John Green and son Frank and Jonathan Thomas. The men's bodies were removed to Silverton where a large funeral was conducted to honor the lost souls.[53]

Two men were running a tunnel for the Silverton Tunnel Company at Grey Copper Falls in Ouray County when they came up missing. Jack

Munroe had gone to the men's cabin but found no sign of them. When he reported the missing men in Silverton a search party was formed composed of Dan M. Dana, Niel Williams, and James Robin who immediately left to learn of the men's fate. They arrived at the mouth of the tunnel and found it covered by rock and debris. Broken timber lay everywhere mixed in with snow. The entrance timbers were broken and the entrance caved-in. No sign of the men could be discerned. After searching the debris for many hours the searchers concluded that the men would be found only when spring melt cleared the area of snow. They concluded that the men had set a charge inside the tunnel and had made it to the entrance when the blast took place. The adit was not yet driven very deep so the blast violently disturbed the entrance causing an avalanche that swept the men into the gulch. The cabin appeared undisturbed with bread mostly baked and the table set for the evening meal. Apparently the men had returned to the cabin to prepare for the evening and then gone back to the mine to finish laying a charge. The men killed were Peter Mulford and Hermon Schrober.[54] Their bodies were found the first week of July.[55]

Denver and Rio Grande train entering an avalanche tunnel below Silverton in Animas Canyon. (Denver Public Library, Western History Department)

In the vicinity of Highland Mary in Cunningham Gulch Andrew Bennie and a friend traveled from the Bonanza Tunnel to Animas Forks when they set off a slide and were buried ten feet deep. Bennie was unable to move, and being tightly encased, believed death would soon follow. Presently he lost consciousness and after a time revived to find himself and his companion lying on top of the snow. A second slide had run and stripped away the first leaving the men shaken, but alive and only slightly injured.[56]

A mail carrier, J. Sellers, and Silverton attorney Fred W. Gardner died in an avalanche at Deep Creek set off by the horses they rode. The bodies were found beneath four feet of snow.[57]

Chalk Ranche was located eight miles north of Leadville in the shadow of Homestake Peak. In 1880 a miner named Gavin came to this lonely desolate spot, located a claim, and went to digging. Railroad construction reached the ranch giving Gavin some weeks of companionship with railroad crews. Construction eventually pushed the rails to the north leaving Gavin alone. One evening Gavin staggered into the little hotel near Birdseye and fell prostrate on the floor. Examination showed his hands, arms and legs to be terribly frozen. His story of suffering almost beyond human endurance unfolded. A week earlier he had sat reading before his cabin fireplace. A storm raged outside. Around ten p.m. he heard a noise like a roaring cataract. Instantly, he felt a short concussion and a crash that made him jump with terror. The earth seemed to shake to its foundation. When Gavin recovered he groped for matches. Finding some, he struck a light to find the door. It could not be moved. He realized an avalanche had buried the cabin. The fire out, midnight darkness surrounded him. He couldn't keep a fire going because the snow buried the smokestack and smoke would fill the cabin. In desperation he started digging a tunnel through the avalanche. Days passed, and with his hands frozen numb, he finally broke through and saw stars shimmering in the clear cold air. Wild with joy, but too weak to shout for help, Gavin crawled back inside and collapsed. He woke up the next day sick and unable to move. Finally, at four p.m. he crawled out and managed to make it to the hotel. He told his story, but his strength would not hold. They buried Gavin six days later.[58]

The season of 1883-1884 is recorded as the winter that produced the greatest number of fatalities. The season also recorded the most deadly single avalanche event at a railroad community in the Gunnison Country.

CHAPTER 2

Avalanche Winter:
1883-1884

> *People of today do not realize how hardy men had to be to live in a steamy, smelly bunkhouse with 200 or more grimy men in damp clothes coming and going continually with hob nailed boots and with no place to go other than down that wet shaft to the bunkhouse or boardinghouse or outdoors into 10 or 12 feet of snowslides and work 10 hours with heavy hand tools.* — Mr. J. T. Pierson, 1940[59]

Mining reached its height during the 1880s. This may account for the winter of 1883-1884 being the deadliest avalanche season in Colorado's history. Over fifty people are estimated to have died. That winter experienced heavier than normal snowfall but was not the year of greatest snowfall. That year occurred fifteen years later during the 1898-1899 winter season. Mining was well developed anywhere valuable minerals were found. Railroads connected every portion of the state. These routes passed over spectacular ranges and through deep canyons. Miners walked, rode horses or mules, and skied to mines which were perched in high valleys and near the summits of peaks. The winter of 1883-1884 produced the single most deadly avalanche event, but everywhere the toll was high.

During the boom days Leadville attracted many more prospectors and miners than could be supported by mineral finds. After gulches were claimed and no other prospects could be found little encouragement was needed for areas beyond the Continental Divide to attract attention. Aspen, Gunnison Country, and the San Juans received an influx of prospectors looking for another Leadville. Few paid any attention to the fact that permanent settlement was denied to these lands, because they were reserved by treaty to the Ute Indians.

Before "silver fever" brought armies of miners the Utes occupied this region for countless generations. By treaty Whites were to stay out of lands west of the 107 degrees longitude. Even if Whites could legally occupy these lands, other factors limited settlement. Difficult weather, slowness obtaining supplies and the remote wilderness kept settlement limited. Then came Leadville's carbonate silver strikes in 1878-1879. It took little time for good prospects to be claimed around Leadville. Just across the divide a possible new bonanza might be waiting. Miners poured over the Sawatch Range and soon found rich deposits. Strikes first occurred along the Roaring Fork River.

Long before settlement, and before the town of Aspen existed, Utes occupied the Roaring Fork Valley. Ute legend said the Roaring Fork River "roared" during spring runoff to punish the people for their indiscretions. When settlers came to the Roaring Fork they named one of the towns Ute City. Illegal settlement and a government agent soon brought relations between Whites and Utes to a tragic confrontation.

At the White River Agency agent Nathan Meeker crusaded to convert the Utes to a settled Christian existence. As a minister and former administrator of the Greeley colony, Meeker viewed his Indian charges as children and in need of salvation. Disagreements quickly developed. The Northern Utes took a dislike to Meeker and his methods. Utes mostly enjoyed hunting and horseracing and had little interest in becoming farmers. After many attempts to rein in the Utes and make them farmers one incident brought the issue to a crisis. Meeker ordered an employee to plow up the racetrack. A rebellion quickly developed. Meeker and the agency's White male employees were killed. A stake was driven through Meeker's mouth so that he wouldn't talk so much in the afterlife. The Army received word of the massacre and a column of soldiers started south from Wyoming. Twenty-five miles from the agency a war party confronted the soldiers. Several casualties occurred on both sides. At the Agency the Utes kidnapped Meeker's wife and the other women and started south. Chief Ouray managed to intervene, convincing the errant Utes to surrender. This incident brought cries from the settlers to remove the Utes from Colorado. They were subsequently forced onto a reservation in Utah and Ute City became Aspen.

Rich silver lode discoveries followed quickly after the strikes at Leadville. Thomas E. Ashcroft surveyed and laid out a new town christened Ashcroft. Even Colorado's Silver King, Horace Tabor, considered Ashcroft prominent enough to bring his bride Baby Doe from Leadville to live while he looked for mining investments.[60] Later, the Tenth Mountain Division, skiing soldiers in World War II, trained in the area, and the 1950s film "Sergeant Preston of the Yukon," was produced there.[61] Aspen emerged as Pitkin County seat in 1881, and Ashcroft fell to second place in significance. When the silver crash hit in 1893 only fifty people lived in Ashcroft.[62] The White Death plagued some mines supporting Ashcroft and Aspen. Aspen's location at the base of Aspen Mountain and the rugged and high Elk Mountains placed it near avalanche paths. A tragic avalanche came down Aspen Mountain above town in 1884. The *Leadville Herald-Democrat* lamented the tragedy:

> *Snowfall and high winds pounded Aspen for several days and gave birth to the worst storm remembered in Roaring Fork Valley. Within three days four feet of snow fell. This new snow piled upon older snowpack loading it to dangerous levels. In places the snow depth reached ten feet.*

On Aspen Mountain, a miner left the Durant Mine to ski into Aspen. On the way he passed the Vallejo Mine. It was obvious that an avalanche had covered the shaft house and mine opening. The miner knew it had trapped many men inside. Hurrying to Aspen, he recruited a large force who made their way up Aspen Mountain to free the miners. When rescuers came to the Vallejo Mine, they saw newly appointed Superintendent, Captain George W. Thatcher extricating himself and other officials.

Captain Thatcher recounted that he and a few other officials descended into the Vallejo Mine leaving the rest at the entrance. Inside they heard a dull thud and snow came crashing into the shaft. Shafts and tunnels protected everyone inside, but they feared for those on the surface. Immediately, he and the rest headed to the blocked mine entrance and pulled and hacked away at the sealed entrance. They dug through snow twenty feet deep before seeing light. Other miners arrived with shovels and cleared the shaft opening. They took to digging a trench toward the shaft house, which was completely covered by the avalanche. Eventually four men were found dead and several others injured.[63]

At the same time, an avalanche descended on nearby Carey's Camp in Conundrum Gulch. Carey's Camp boomed the previous summer with more than a hundred miners scouring the hills. Several new mines produced valuable ores. Most people left Conundrum Gulch during the severe winter, but a few stayed. Those who decided to stay through the winter realized the danger of the heavy snow and avalanches. They erected a strong, reinforced cabin with huge logs and well-secured beams to resist snow loading and avalanche hits. These precautions were no match for the awesome power of snow in massive movement as it descended on the opposite side of the gulch and then

> . . . filled up the whole creek with snow, ice, timber, rocks and debris of every kind, and then rushed on up the slope and over a bench for at least 200 feet and crushing in its course the cabin of the boys at work on the Southern Home, and piling up the snow and debris from thirty to fifty feet in all the latter part of its course.[64]

A fracture in the snow at the head of Conundrum Gulch extended a width of 400 feet. The avalanche started high on Conundrum Gulch's west side and descended a full mile. Along its course it gathered tons of snow and debris, which filled the gulch. Its velocity and mass were too great for the narrow valley to contain. Momentum carried the avalanche up the opposite slope from its origin destroying the miners' cabin at Carey's Camp and killing the men inside. No one at nearby camps heard or saw the avalanche.

The storm raged for several days and severed communication between camps. After it ended, J. B. Sparger decided to visit Carey's

Camp and see how the men there had fared throughout the long snow-fall assault. Upon arrival, he scanned the surface and saw that debris-littered snow at least thirty feet deep covered the gulch, cabins, and every human object. Sparger swiftly left for Aspen to organize a rescue party.

He arrived at Aspen just as the funeral services for the Vallejo Mine victims commenced. Thirty volunteers rapidly assembled and were supplied with tools by Henry Gillaspie, Cowenhoven & Co. and others and departed by full moon to find the Carey's Camp victims. They reached their unhappy destination and began trenching and digging without rest until dawn. After cutting through thirty feet of tightly packed snow, tools finally struck the massive cabin walls. The building walls stood intact, but its roof had crashed down upon the unwary inhabitants killing them all. The tragedy was made even more horrible as it had occurred at the moment the day shift had arrived from the mine and before the night crew had left. The five men killed were Samuel Steele, Joseph Steele, George Morris, J. F. Thorne and J. T. Tate.

The rescuers recovered the bodies, wrapped them in deerskins, and pulled them on sleds into Aspen. Many owners closed their mines and sent their workers to town to wait for safer conditions.[65] Twelve men died in the Aspen and Ashcroft area by the end of the 1883-1884 avalanche season.[66]

A year later the *Aspen Times* printed a short memorial for men caught at Vallejo and Carey's Camp.

> *Well must everyone remember the frantic cry which amidst the terrific storm rent the air that seventeen brave and noble men of the mountains lie buried beneath an avalanche of snow, which had slid down the mountain sides and landed upon the shaft house of the Vallejo Mine. In less time than it takes to tell nearly three hundred men were climbing that great mountainside amid sleet and snow with shovels, picks, drills and gas pipes, willing to do all in their power to relieve their suffering comrades. Yesterday saw the anniversary of the death of John B. Meginity, George Marshall, William O'Brien and Michael Higgins at the Vallejo, and S. A. Steele, John F. Tate, J. W. Thorne, George Morris and Joseph P. Steele, in the Cary Camp, up Conundrum Gulch. Peace to their ashes. Everyone in Pitkin County reveres their memory.[67]*

Other gulches produced injury and death during the season. A snowslide in Queen's Gulch killed a well-known Aspen man. John Riser, Castle Rock Mining Company foreman, and Charles Miller had started from Queen's Gulch for Aspen. An avalanche caught Riser as it swept into Queen's Gulch. The search lasted an hour before they found Riser's body. Another time a report brought many rescuers to look for James Mason who was also caught in a Queen's Gulch slide. Mason, an early pioneer of Aspen's mineral rush, had various properties under development. Probing went on several hours before searchers uncovered his body. In early winter on November 25, 1883, Charlie Davis, a property owner in Conundrum Gulch, and a companion climbed to the Rainstorm Mine near Ashcroft for the night shift. A massive avalanche caught and carried them 200 feet. Although completely buried, Keeley dug himself out. Searchers gathered to look for Charlie Davis who was found dead.

About twelve miles north of Grand Lake in Bowen Gulch a slide struck at the Topinis Mine in February 1883. Charles Rogers and John Stokes had made their way to the mine on horses, but deep snow slowed their progress. For the last three miles of the trip the men had to dismount and trudge through the snow with the horses in tow. Just as they sighted the cabins and buildings at the mine an avalanche flew in carrying everything away. The delay along the route saved their lives. They knew that some other miners might have been at the mine so they went to the Wolverine Mine for help. By the next day they recovered three bodies at the Topinis.[68]

Swan Nilson, who carried mail on long skis between Silverton and Ophir in the San Juans, disappeared around Christmas in 1883 near Ophir Pass.[69] He started out from Silverton on December 23, 1883, in a raging snowstorm carrying Christmas gifts and money for the residents of Ophir. His friends tried to stop him from making the perilous journey through avalanche country, but Nilson was true to his calling that the mail must get through. When he failed to arrive, a search party went out from Ophir but no sign of Nilson could be found. They searched for several days and finally gave him up for lost in the unforgiving mountains. Summer came, the snow melted and friends continued the search. Again no sign of Nilson and rumors began to fly that maybe he had taken the large amount of cash he carried and left the country. Friends persisted believing that Nilson was honest and would never dream of taking Christmas from anyone. Twenty months later his body turned up deep in a gulch buried under a snowbank that had been overlooked. On his back the mailbag was securely attached, and when the bag was cut open the money and presents were secure.[70]

Sneffels is one of Colorado's 14,000-foot peaks. Its name comes from the mountain in Jules Vernes' *Journey to the Center of the Earth*.[71] As early prospectors staked claims through the San Juans a few went to the vicinity of Mt. Sneffels where they discovered several important mines. These included the Yankee Boy, Wheel of Fortune, Ruby Trust and the richest of all — the Virginius.

Mining at the Virginius began in 1876. Several men spent the winter working the mine at an altitude of 12,600 feet. Nearly every morning they dug through deep snowdrifts from the boardinghouse to daylight. In the spring the miners packed out twenty-one tons of ore. Their efforts brought $8,000 — a large sum for the day. When offered a small fortune for the mine they sold out in 1877. Over the next few years output increased.[72] The silver crash in 1893 closed most mines, but because of the Virginius' rich silver ore with its high gold content it continued operating. In 1895 the Revenue Tunnel was driven. It ran 7,500 feet into the mountain and started some 2,000 feet below the tunnels of Virginius. Shafts provided ventilation and drainage. The Virginius's already huge operation expanded to employ over 600 miners.[73] Its post office was thought to be the highest ever established in the country.

On December 21, 1883, mail carrier Al Sophy arrived in Ouray and brought news of a disaster at the Virginius while he was completing his rounds in the Sneffels District. The Virginius was one of the highest mines in the San Juans and considered safer than most since it stood so close to the mountain summits that not very much snow would be brought down if a slide ran. For this reason, few in Ouray believed the story until checking with General Manager H. W. Reed who confirmed that he had also just received word of the avalanche. Patrick Quinn, who worked at the Virginius, risked his life to bring news of the disaster to Reed in Ouray. During his dash to report the disaster he skied through Cumberland Basin and minutes later he heard a slide come down at a location he had just passed. He arrived in the afternoon on Saturday the day after the slide. Reed, his brother David, Quinn, and a few others mounted horses and started for the Virginius. When they reached Richardson's cabin later that evening the horses were sheltered and the men continued on skis, but the storm so hindered travel that they stopped for the night at Porter's store to wait for daybreak. A reporter for the *Solid Muldoon* who first accompanied the men went back to Ouray to arrange for receiving the dead and aiding the injured and to organize parties to check on miners feared to be in danger.

For the previous three days snowfall had been heavy and snowslides ran one after another making the earth tremble. It was feared that many isolated camps or cabins might be buried and their occupants killed. M. Parmody and P. Henessy left their cabin early in the morning when an immense slide covered the cabin. The men continued on their journey, but when they passed the location of the cabin of John Sheldon and John Sullivan they saw it lay buried under snow up to fifty feet deep, with the roof crushed in and the men probably dead. At Silver Creek there was concern for the five men who worked there although it was believed that the cabin was safely located, but as learned at the Virginius, no location could be called safe.

The Virginius avalanche started about 150 feet above the buildings and boardinghouse at about 4:30 in the afternoon. As it ran, tons of additional snow were picked up and carried along adding to its destructive force. When it hit the boardinghouse twelve men were inside. Thomas Mursen, Robert Frazier, Thomas Fitzgerald and W. K. Carmichael who slept at the east end of the building died instantly. The others all survived. The roof had been crushed to the floor and snow-packed in hard as ice. The force opened a hole in the office where Edward Boyle the foreman worked allowing his escape. He rushed into the mine and returned with the seventeen miners working the drifts. Upon arriving at the disaster, the men set to work picking and shoveling away the avalanche and within fifteen minutes pulled William Collins out of the wreckage bruised but not seriously injured. Just five minutes later Patrick Fadden was dug out, cut on the forehead, but not seriously hurt. John Vanola saw light forty-five minutes after Fadden, followed soon after by Giuseppe Perotti. Unconscious when found, Perotti was taken to the engine room, stripped, and hot clothing applied to revive him from hypothermia. After an hour of this treatment he revived enough to speak. Thomas O'Connor had been buried under fifteen feet of snow and debris for over an hour when found. Snow was so tightly packed around him that all he could do was breathe. He managed to call out which alerted searchers to his location. With O'Connor found and safely removed to a warm location only Charles Armstrong and William H. Shidler remained missing. Searchers believed they lay buried under fifty feet of snow in the gulch below. Searching continued in the gulch until midnight when they retreated to the ore house for the night.

The next day the searchers had no food or provisions, so foreman Boyle instructed the men to dig to the kitchen and cellar in the boardinghouse from the portion of the office still standing. In the early afternoon they reached the cellar, broke in, and to their surprise found Charles Armstrong and Will Shidler alive and well. Armstrong said that when the slide hit it pinned them against the wall in the kitchen about three feet from the cellar door. He said that he had some breathing space and could move enough to use a board and force open an air channel to Shidler. With adequate air the relieved men began digging themselves out. They could hear the work going on overhead but their cries were never heard. Digging toward the stove Armstrong came across the coffee boiler that contained some of the lukewarm beverage. The men satisfied themselves and used the rest to help melt the snow. Realizing the search for them had ended for the night, Armstrong decided that they should reach the cellar where other provisions could be found. They dug until 2 a.m. using pieces of boards and shingle from roof debris. When the men reached the cellar they emptied bags of vegetables and used the burlap bags to keep themselves warm until morning.[74]

Soon after wrapping the bodies in canvas and securing them to sleds teams of skiers started off to Ouray from the Virginius Mine. Soon after this picture was taken more than thirty rescuers were caught in a slide. All survived but the sleds were buried. (Denver Public Library, Western History Department)

On Christmas Eve David Day, the *Solid Muldoon* newspaper editor, Manager Reed, David Reed, and the others reached the site to help rescue and care for the injured. After a visit to the disaster site the men went to the Monongahela where the dead and injured had been taken. They prepared the dead bodies and the severely injured for transport. Two large, rudely built sleds were made to carry two bodies each. Miners' advocate David Day went back to Ouray in a heavy storm and readied the town to receive the injured and dead. Thirty-two men from the Virginius and Monongahela pulled the sleds by a long rope fastened to the front. They started making their way down the steep road to Ouray. David Reed broke trail and others kept eyes and ears tuned for signs of avalanches starting. All agreed that Cumberland Basin presented the greatest danger. If they got through the basin the remainder of the trip would be relatively safe. The moment the funeral procession reached Cumberland Basin the hillside slid lifting David Reed into the air and over a precipice. A second slide followed the first and carried off the other thirty-one men and sleds. Foreman Edward Boyle freed himself first and looked around at this latest disaster. An eerie scene of hands and feet, some moving, protruded everywhere from debris. He worked feverishly and before long freed several men who were alive. In turn, survivors dug for others. Some had gone over the precipice 500 feet down. In one of the most amazing avalanche stories ever, all were found and none seriously injured. The sleds were another matter. They were

Two of the Virginius Mine fatalities on the way to Ouray several weeks after the 1883 avalanche that killed four. (Colorado Historical Society)

not seen on the surface during the quick search that ensued. After a time all were convinced that remaining in the area courted disaster. Each man chose to return either to town or the Virginius to wait for a time when recovery of the sleds could resume.[75] Four men who had been carried farthest down lost their skis and had to retreat to the Governor cabins until they could recover from shock and return to look for the skis.

After this disaster the company provided safer conditions for winter mining. They reopened the Virginius and mined it for several more decades. In 1897 tunnels reached the level of the Revenue Tunnel nearly 2000 feet below. From then on miners entered the workings from the Revenue adits that are at a much lower altitude and safer location.[76]

The day after the Virginius avalanche a slide overtook Mendota Mine near Telluride. Several men were in the shaft house preparing skis for the run to Telluride for Christmas when at about four in the afternoon a slide started near the top of the divide above the mine. The slide carried away everything and everyone in and around the shaft house including three horses, thirteen hundred pounds of giant powder, hay, grain, provisions, mining implements, and the fifteen men at the shaft house for a distance of 600 feet. The eight killed were J. H. Bond, C. S. Herrick, Thomas Donegan, W. M. Taylor, John Davis, William Applewhite, Lewis Hutchinson, and Fergus Slater. Several others were injured to varying degrees. The slide missed the boardinghouse sparing the lives of the nine men inside. It continued on, reaching the edge of the Sheridan boardinghouse where its strength dissipated. The eight victims of the Mendota received a large ceremony and burial by the people of Telluride.

Other mines in the region had visits by the White Death. At the Gold Bug, James Burns and Scotty Furquharson died without struggle when an avalanche buried their cabin. Days before the big storm began the Gold Bug Mine was sold by owners Barney Mallon and James Burns. Before starting for their homes, Mallon to Lake City and Burns for Pueblo, the men determined to return to the Gold Bug and make the mine ready for the transfer. Then the great snowstorm started, and Mallon, sensing danger, tried to convince Burns and Fred "Scotty" Farquharson to descend to the safer Cincinnati Mine. The men scoffed at Mallon but he left for the Cincinnati anyway.

All that night Mallon heard the crash and boom of avalanches. Two days later Mallon decided to go check on the men at the Gold Bug. When he reached the site the cabin was gone and he began digging for the unfortunate men. For two more days he dug until he found Burns standing as if he had heard the slide coming and had risen to try to escape. The snow was melted from around his body and he was still quite warm indicating that he had lived almost up until the time Mallon found him. The same roof timber that fell and killed Furquharson apparently broke Burns' wrist.

In grief but with determination to bring his friends' bodies out Mallon offered $200 to anyone who would help him remove the bodies to Telluride. The danger was so great that everyone refused. Mallon carried Burns and Farquharson on his back down the gulch for 4,000 feet alternately breaking a path through the deep snow and then climbing back up to retrieve the bodies. Facing death at every step Mallon continued his merciful endeavor until he reached Telluride where the bodies could be properly prepared for burial. He then sent Burns's body to Montrose where the dead man's brothers arrived from Pueblo to claim the body. Relatives claimed Furquharson's body which was was buried at Telluride where they all lived.[77]

At the Nevada near Ophir two men died in similar circumstances to those at the Gold Bug.[78]

The "Gunnison Country" received its name from the leader of a government survey party named John W. Gunnison who mapped and explored a route for a wagon road and possible railroad route from the east to the Pacific. He passed through the Gunnison Country in 1853, but was killed by Paiutes at Sevier Lake in Utah.[79] The surviving explorers finished their mission to California. Twenty years later Sylvester Richardson established a colony near where the United States government managed a cow camp to provide cattle for the Ute Los Pinos Agency in Saguache County. Most colonists eventually left, but a few remained attracted by the possibilities of agriculture and mineral development. Gunnison County was created from Saguache County in 1877. John Evans, Sylvester Richardson, Alonzo Hartman and others established the Gunnison City Town Company in 1879 and platted the site. Two railroads began pushing rails through central Colorado — the Denver South Park and Pacific and the Denver and Rio Grande with Gunnison as an important destination. A rivalry developed over which railroad would be first to push through central Colorado. General Palmer's Rio Grande arrived first in 1881 having been built over Otto Mears's right-of-way of Marshall Pass. The South Park line experienced difficulty driving the Alpine Tunnel above St. Elmo. Loose rather than hard rock plagued the work and required expensive shoring of the tunnel walls over nearly its entire length. The South Park steamed into Gunnison a year later in 1882. Evans' grandiose plans to build or connect to the Pacific shores ended north of Gunnison at the Baldwin coal fields. Gunnison thrived and became the hub of mining, stock raising, and agriculture in the region. Many predicted Gunnison would become a center for steel manufacturing, smelter operations, and a mining supply point rivaling Leadville, but these hopes never materialized. Severe winters, high transportation costs, and the lack of rich carbonate ores conspired to limit Gunnison's growth. But, served by two railroads, Gunnison survived as a supply center for mining and agriculture.[80]

Winter anywhere in the Colorado Rockies means cold and snow, but Gunnison frequently records the lowest average winter temperatures in the Continental United States. Of all valleys and basins of the Gunnison Country, Taylor Park holds the record at minus 56 degrees Fahrenheit. This Western Slope valley at an altitude of over 8,000 feet is snowbound all winter with snow six or more feet deep on the flat.[81] In 1861 Fred Lottis spent a summer prospecting for gold in the area on the stream later named for him. At Union Park he discovered gold using a tin cup, and Tincup City received one of the West's most colorful names. That same year Utes killed several prospectors after a three-day battle. The name of Dead Man's Gulch memorializes this fight.[82] Tincup and Taylor Park thrived from 1880 to 1883 and then declined.

Northwest of Taylor Park the town of Crested Butte also has deep snows. Travelers along roads in summer noted wagon wheel scars twenty-five feet high on trees made the previous winter season. Crested Butte is famous for its two-story outhouses — the upper floor easily reached in winter. Founded on gold discovered in the area, Crested Butte later became a supply town and stop for Aspen-to-Gunnison travelers. High quality coal deposits fed railroads and smelters and sustained its economy into the 1950s.

In western Gunnison County the Denver South Park and Pacific Railroad fought snow and avalanches along its route from St. Elmo to Pitkin. Slides often ran and blocked the grade on both the Atlantic and Pacific sides of Alpine Tunnel. Everywhere heavy snows and cold temperatures made the mining areas in Gunnison County particularly dangerous.

Several lamentable avalanche disasters unfolded in Gunnison County. In January 1884, near Crested Butte, the mine owners left to ski into town. As they passed the Venango Mine dump, Michael Lawler on webbed shoes, and Thomas Owens on skis set loose a slide. A fracture line started at the Belmont adit above. Snowpack cracked horizontally for a length of a thousand feet encompassing thousands of tons of snow. The avalanche carried Lawler and Owens along with a lot of other debris. When it stopped, Owens was buried under the snow, but he still had his ski pole in hand. He managed to poke an air hole through to the surface with the pole. With great effort, Owens frantically freed himself. He searched for Lawler with no luck. Owens went to get help at Crested Butte. Searchers returned and worked all night and into the next afternoon before Lawler's body was found at the edge of Elk Creek. No ice mask had formed on his face, suggesting Michael Lawler died that January while the slide remained in motion.

The last day of January, at four a.m., thirty men inside the Anthracite Coal Mine boardinghouse heard a slide. They had no time to seek safety. The avalanche hit, hurling the building and all its contents down the mountainside. It killed six and seriously wounded fifteen.[83] Another catastrophe preceded this calamity the day before at Ruby-Irwin Mine, just west of Anthracite Coal Mine.

Near Floresta, the Ruby-Irwin Mine grew fast and died even faster. In 1879, three mines opened containing rich ore called ruby silver. Miners staked many more claims by the fall of that year. The first winter fifty feet of snow fell covering all of the buildings. Citizens dug tunnels between cabins and buildings to communicate and exchange goods. Someone trying to find Irwin observed from the road that it should be called Mole City. When spring came tons of goods were stockpiled at the gulch's head to wait for the time when the gulch road became passable. Merchants paid men extremely well to haul perishables on their backs the short and difficult distance up the gulch. These loads weighed from one to two hundred pounds. Men began hauling at three a.m. before a warming sun had a chance to soften the hard snow crust.[84]

Ruby Mountain above Irwin threatened several mines with avalanches. On January 30, 1883, a slide overtook the Durango, Ruby Chief, Oaks, Old Sheik and Howard Extension mines carrying away shaft houses and other buildings. Several men lay buried beneath wide and deep avalanche debris. Searchers found all but two men at the Howard Extension alive. They were safely inside the workings when the slide ran. Frank Ranander died at the scene and Tom Brown later died of injuries.[85]

The "snowshoe" mail carrier's perilous life became known time and again in the West's mountainous regions. Carrier A. C. Adair regularly skied the distance from Crested Butte to Aspen. He came up missing in March 1885. A search party found his body on the Ashcroft side of avalanche-prone Pearl Pass.[86]

Tomichi City, near Tomichi Creek's headwaters in eastern Gunnison County, experienced several serious avalanches. On February 2, 1883, a slide struck Tomichi City and wiped away nine log cabins. Hearing the avalanche coming one owner of a cabin ducked for cover at the dwelling's low side and escaped injury. The roof collapsed, but logs jammed diagonally from roof to floor, protecting him from being crushed by tons of snow and debris. Two miles to the south in White Pine a slide came down, but the lucky miner managed to run into the mine tunnel as the avalanche flowed past.[87] In 1899, the "Year of the Big Snow," a giant avalanche again visited Tomichi.[88]

Two men from Chicago had come out to Colorado and prospected in 1879. Both were ill and came to live out their last days by adventuring in the Wild West. They discovered the Sylvanite lode near

Gothic. Gothic was active from 1879 to 1885 — sustained by the Sylvanite mine and its ore of "wire silver." When United States Government officials sought an example of a lawless rowdy western town for President Grant to visit they chose Gothic.

Snowslides took a heavy toll in property and life at the Elk Mountain Mining District. It encompassed an area including Rock Creek, Brush Creek, Maroon Creek, Rustler Gulch, Washington Gulch, Copper Creek, and across the range into Yule Creek.[89] In Copper Creek, the Sylvanite Mine became the leading silver producer. As miners left each winter day for the mine the women in Gothic told their husbands, brothers, and fathers perhaps their last good-bye for fear that an avalanche, not an unscheduled explosion or cave-in, would bring death.[90]

Anticipating disastrous avalanches, owners gave special consideration in constructing boardinghouse and other surface buildings. The Sylvanite boardinghouse had a steeply pitched roof joined to an excavated hillside. This permitted avalanches to run unobstructed over the building. Slides ran across the boardinghouse after nearly every storm. The boardinghouse, blacksmith shop, and an ore house were connected to the mine by a covered walkway with a roof like the boardinghouse to shed snow. This avalanche construction technique held up well under numerous onslaughts.

All winter in 1883-1884, slides passed harmlessly overhead. In early January, miners heard an enormous avalanche start high above and decided to seek better protection. They quickly retreated into the tunnel through the covered way. As the avalanche passed overhead the substantial log building shook violently. To the men it seemed the buildings:

> . . . *must be ground from their strong foundations by the tremendous weight of ice and snow that was grinding and crunching its way across the log roof. The sides were moved and the roof was sprung down several inches* . . .[91]

After all became quiet they re-entered their living quarters. Outside a storm raged. Inside smoke filled the room. The avalanche had whisked away the stovepipe. Fifteen feet of snow on the boardinghouse roof sealed its opening. Using long ski poles, the men poked and prodded a new hole to allow smoke to escape. The storm and avalanches continued for two days. Whenever they heard a slide's crack or boom, which heralded its start, the men ran to the tunnel and waited for its passage. When all was quiet the miners returned. After opening new air holes, they waited for the next slide. After the storm passed, several more slides passed overhead and then stopped. Digging through thirty feet of snow the miners finally saw daylight.

Eight railroad workers came into Montrose after a tragedy while building the Denver and Rio Grande Railroad through Black Canyon. About five o'clock in the morning a snowslide crashed into camp on top of about forty men still asleep in their tents. It killed three men, eight mules and destroyed the cookhouse. At the same moment, another avalanche descended at the upper end of the camp but missed the men sleeping there. After digging trenches two men were found alive.[92]

While railroad men struggled with slides in Black Canyon west of Gunnison, a disaster took shape in Sawatch Range in eastern Gunnison County. It was surprisingly not in the dangerous San Juan Mountains, the place of many fatal avalanche disasters, but rather in Gunnison County at Woodstock, that the single most deadly avalanche disaster in Colorado happened.

In the wild mountain gulches of Colorado, railroads contested against deep snow and avalanches and of all the central Colorado mountain railroads none contended more than the Denver, South Park and Pacific. Founded by Colorado's second territorial governor, John Evans, the South Park became and is still today, one of the most famous narrow gauge railroads in the world. Railroad buffs everywhere know its name and its legendary history. The South Park crossed through ranges that produced some of the heaviest snows and avalanche conditions in Colorado. The cost of construction and the difficulty of keeping the road open in the winter cut deeply into the operating expenses of the Denver, South Park and Pacific. For this reason the company often operated at a loss.

The engineering marvel of the South Park Line is where it crossed under the Continental Divide through the Alpine Tunnel on its way to the railroad town of Woodstock. It was the first tunnel from the Atlantic to the Pacific side of the continent. Built to the narrow gauge standard, the three-foot-wide track was entirely suited for Colorado Rocky Mountain railroad building. With Colorado having the highest average altitude of any state, railroad builders found a three-foot wide track easier and cheaper to fling up steep mountain ranges, throw across deep chasms, and support against sheer cliff faces. Lower costs for rails, engines, and rolling stock gave further incentives for mountain railroad builders to adopt the narrow gauge over the emerging American standard of four feet, eight-and-a-half inches. Narrow gauge standard allowed for steeper grades and sharper curves lowering costs in cuts, backfill and tunneling.

The Denver, South Park and Pacific originated in Denver and terminated at Baldwin, north of Gunnison. The little railroad passed over some of the highest passes in American railroading — Boreas Pass and the Alpine Tunnel. One branch of the South Park line extended from Como over 12,000-foot-high Boreas Pass, through Breckenridge, and then on to serve Leadville and other mining districts. At the Alpine Tunnel which crosses the great divide between St. Elmo on the east side, and Pitkin on the west, snow and avalanches would close sections of the line for weeks at a time making train movement impossible. Eventually, winter conditions closed portions of the line permanently and contributed to the railroad's demise.

West Portal of Alpine Tunnel with snowsheds and snow fences. At center is Alpine Station, also called Pacific, with its snow shed. The date on the photograph is incorrect. Alpine Tunnel was completed in 1881. (Denver Public Library, Western History Department)

Along the section of track from St. Elmo to Pitkin, the Denver, South Park and Pacific struggled up and down the rugged Sawatch Range. From St. Elmo the narrow gauge passed mostly without incident up a steep grade of four percent, but in the winter, trains bucked snowdrifts all the way. At Hancock the train scheduled a stop. Crew and passengers refreshed at the hotel and then embarked on an avalanche-prone grade for three miles to the east portal that was called "Atlantic." At an altitude of 11,600 feet, the line entered the Alpine Tunnel on a curve bored into the mountainside. It traveled for nearly 1800 feet under the Continental Divide, and reached the "Pacific," or Alpine Station on the Western Slope. The Alpine Station provided an eating place, boarding-house, and engine house with a square water tank inside the building to keep it from freezing and spectacular scenery in a hanging glacial valley. While crews paused to fill the boiler with water, passengers took

Woodstock before the avalanche. (Denver Public Library, Western History Department)

a break and then reboarded for the descent to Pitkin. This part of the journey brought into view some of the most striking Rocky Mountain scenery. Green forests grew far down in the valley. Treeless tundra on the mountain peaks interspersed with color splashes from the sudden growth of flowers in the short summer season. Hillsides turned brilliant orange and red in fall before shimmering snow colored the ground white. Shortly after Alpine Station, the train stopped at the Palisades. The Palisades are a sheer cliff face that required construction of a massive rock wall against the cliff to hold the grade and track. Passengers often disembarked to see this marvel of railroad engineering. Leaving Palisades the train clattered down around Sherrod Loop and stopped at Woodstock.

The railroad established Woodstock to service their employees and trains. Woodstock started out as a construction camp when rails reached there in 1881. They eventually built a depot, telegraph office, section house, water tank, hotel, saloon, car shed, workshop, eating place, and a few cabins. A 500-foot-long spur provided a place to park cars filled with materials. Railroad workers unloaded supplies from freight cars into wagons heading down to Pitkin.[93] Contractors and employees who were building the railroad from this point to Pitkin lived at Woodstock. After the rails reached Pitkin, Woodstock became a permanent settlement. Workers stripped trees from slopes above Woodstock for railroad ties, building materials and firewood.[94]

On March 10, 1884, recently widowed Mrs. Marcella Doyle from Golden managed the boardinghouse at Woodstock with the help of six of her eight children. She was busy all day caring for passengers and workers. Down the street the telegraph operator J. S. Brown worked at sending railroad and private business messages. From his window he could see blowing snow coming down in spirals. Meanwhile, heavy snow and drifting blocked the Rio Grande line over Marshall Pass, several miles south, leaving the South Park as the only rail route open to Denver.

A dozen miles south, across Tomichi Pass at White Pine, Eugene Teats showed mining claims to two possible investors. The snowstorm had started the day before and continued dumping heavy snowfall as the men prepared to leave for Woodstock to catch a train for Denver. Riding ponies, the three had a final look at the claims and then reined their horses toward Tomichi Pass. Deep snow covered all but a faint trace of the rocky road. Whiteout conditions almost blinded them. Reaching the top of the pass, they surveyed several routes to Woodstock. The men could follow a road that wound along the mountainside for several miles or they could force a way through directly down untracked snow. They selected the direct route that cut the distance in half but contained some risk. The horses were trained to return by themselves to White Pine, so they turned them back toward home and the men started down the pass. Their walk became a matter of survival. Taking turns, each man broke trail through the waste-deep snowpack. They struggled to make the last stretch, each step sinking deeper into the powdery snow slowing their journey toward Woodstock. Wind whipped and chilled them almost beyond endurance. Teats and his partners were about to give up when the wind suddenly stopped. Woodstock loomed only a short distance away and the vision renewed their strength. They ran, stumbling their way into Mrs. Doyle's eating house and a sense of safety. Outside heavy snow, wind, and steep slopes added up to extreme avalanche conditions.

Crude sleds fashioned from lumber with runners composed of flat iron secured to timber runners have received their cargo for the ten mile run to Pitkin. (Grant Houston Collection, Lake City)

After a meal and hot coffee, the three heard "all aboard" and the men climbed on the train. Behind schedule, the train embarked on the first part of the journey to the Alpine Tunnel. Entering the Pullman car, the men settled in for the trip as the train rounded Sherrod Curve and began the three-mile ascent to the Alpine Tunnel. Sherrod Loop brought the train around 180 degrees from a southerly to northerly direction while passing above Woodstock. Stacked beside the track were large timbers and heavy flat boards for a snowshed. In an instant disaster struck. Years later, Teats described what he saw from the train that day:

> *. . . off we started on the upgrade toward where we had just come from, only on the opposite side of the gulch. Here we could look across to the awful peril we had so recently left. We had to go quite a way up Missouri Gulch to gain the necessary grade to take us over Altman Pass (Alpine Tunnel). We had not been long on the return switchback and well out of the gulch up on the mountainside, before we stalled in a deep cut filled with snow packed so hard that our double header could not buck its way through. It was then we beheld the most alarming sights I have ever experienced. The air became surcharged with snow, so fine, so dense, simply a snow fog without the foghorn, and the crashing and roaring like the tearing away of the mountainside.*
>
> *Looking from the windows and doors we could see a moving mass. The whole mountain side seemed sliding into, and filling up the gulch, and it was then that we realized how lately we had left the very spot, or side of the mountain from which this great avalanche of snow had come. . . . The great body of snow moved with the speed of "air birds" (air-planes) of this day. Finally it reached the railroad level and had seemingly selected for its stopping and final resting the place the very spot where we had so recently boarded the Pullman at Woodstock station.*
>
> *. . . The overpowering avalanche of snow had done its death dealing work, and had swept everything before it, taking rocks, trees, bushes — everything from the top of the mountain to the bottom, leaving in its wake a bare swath. . . . We on the train did not dream of the fate of those who had lately ministered to our wants.*[95]

The train Teats rode backed up to get a run at drifts ahead, then slammed into the drifts, making only a few feet at a time. All night this continued until it reached the tunnel, only three and a half miles from Woodstock. Beyond the Alpine Tunnel, the going was easier to Hancock, where warm coffee and a meal awaited passengers and crew. After refreshment and taking on water, the train pulled away for an uneventful trip to Denver.

All this time, the whole truth of the disaster was unknown to Teats. The avalanche had completely buried Woodstock including section house, telegraph office, all railroad buildings, and several dwellings and destroyed the substantial water tank.[96] People speculated heavy boards placed along the upper grade on the bare hillside, accompanied with huge boulders and the few remaining trees yanked from the ground, added deadly mass to the avalanche as it rushed to Woodstock and Missouri Gulch.[97]

First news of the catastrophe came from a man who dug himself out and managed to make it to Pitkin ten miles distant.[98] The alarm went out by telegraph up and down the line. Word of the disaster reached Superintendent Smith who ordered twenty-five men from Alpine Tunnel to descend to the slide area and begin searching. Smith sent a telegraph to notify others of the disaster — " . . . a terrible snowslide occurred at six o'clock last evening at Woodstock, on the South Park road, three miles west of the Alpine Tunnel."[99]

On the way to Pitkin with bodies of the Woodstock avalanche in 1884. (Grant Houston Collection, Lake City)

Thirty volunteers from Pitkin assembled and skied to Woodstock. Volunteers dug a long trench and probed with sticks in the snow in the hope of intersecting victims. They quickly found five victims alive. Rescuers continued the difficult and emotional work for two days before ten of the thirteen missing were found. Searchers persisted several more days, when they finally discovered two additional children. Months later a newspaper account related that:

> *. . . Those rescued alive were Mrs. Doyle, Hugh Alexander, Peter Wallpole, Walter Hoyt, and Mrs. Doyle's niece, Miss Celia Dillon. Miss Dillon is found standing among some timbers beneath where the snow has held her for over fifteen hours. Rescuers found Mrs. Doyle a few hours before . . . Others killed were George Alexander, Michael Shea, Jasper Caswell, and James Tracy.*[100]

Building destroyed by the Woodstock avalanche. (Grant Houston Collection, Lake City)

Mrs. Doyle's children were Martin, Andrew, Katie, Marcellis, Maggie, and Christopher. Two more bodies were found days later. Spring came late to the mountains and gave up its frozen grip only grudgingly on the final missing man. Only in June was the saloon keeper Joe Royegno found.

Makeshift sleds, pulled by teams of skiers, transported the bodies to a morgue ten miles away in Pitkin. The trip to Pitkin threatened rescuers as the sleds bogged down and powdery drifts sloughed off and threatened massive slides at any moment. Several times sleds overturned dumping bodies into drifts requiring more searching to find the victim. In the distance, booms could be heard as natural avalanches ran.

After days of backbreaking work with explosives, picks shovels the rail is finally reached. Woodstock avalanche, 1884. (Grant Houston Collection, Lake City)

Mrs. Doyle, whose husband had died in 1880 leaving her penniless, lost six of her eight children. Moving from Golden only months before, Mrs. Doyle agreed to run the boardinghouse and cook meals for the South Park division of Union Pacific.[101] She later filed in United States Court to recover damages for her losses:

> *Mrs. Marcella Doyle who lost [most of] her . . . family of three sons and three daughters, brought suit in the United States Court against the Denver South Park & Pacific to recover $50,000 . . . Her three boys were 23, 19, and 10 years old respectively, while her three daughters were 18, 14, and 12 years old. Mrs. Doyle contends that she was induced by the railroad company to take charge of the boardinghouse at Woodstock near which place the company had a large force of men at work. Mrs. Doyle contends that she and the girls cooked and that her three boys worked for the railroad. She contends that the Woodstock station was built directly in the path of where numerous snowslides had occurred, but of this fact, she alleges, she was kept in ignorance . . . She states that she depended on her children for*

support, and by their loss she is left without means. The aged Mother claims $5,000 for each child and $20,000 for injuries and damages to herself and personal property.[102]

The result of the ruling is unknown. Mrs. Doyle returned to Golden with her two surviving children.[103] She outlived both.

They never rebuilt Woodstock. Later, railroad owners extended the spur and built a bunkhouse in the vicinity. A square water tank, placed on Williams Pass Creek, a half mile to the west, replaced the one destroyed at Woodstock.[104] In 1909, another giant slide came down in the same place with no injury or loss of life. It took seven days to clear this slide and reopen the line. The Woodstock avalanche of March 10, 1884, remains the single most deadly snowslide in Colorado history, killing thirteen people.[105]

Foundation of the Woodstock tank destroyed in the 1884 avalanche that killed thirteen people. At upper center the husky, Denali, drinks from the waterpipe that still delivers water from the spring above. (J. W. Jenkins Photo)

To see the Woodstock avalanche site, drive three miles north of Pitkin and ascend the grade beginning at the site of Quartz toward the Alpine Tunnel. Watch for signage describing various sites along the way, until reaching Woodstock about six miles up the grade just before Sherrod Loop. Visitors can easily see the original tank's foundation, its iron pipe still spouting water, next to the grade.

CHAPTER 3

The First Mining Disaster was Caused by an Avalanche: Homestake

> *". . . An avalanche at Homestake Mine had engulfed the whole workforce employed at that point. When the event occurred is unknown, but the bodies of the men bear evidence of having been long covered by the weighty death mantle."* — Summit County Journal [106]

In 1860, Granite, twenty miles south of Leadville, had already gained a reputation as a place with good gold placer deposits. Placer mining is the cheapest and easiest form of gold mining, requiring nothing more than picks, shovels, a sluice box, and a strong back. Placers are gold deposits on the surface in streams and along stream banks. Sluices are long boxes with ribs placed across the bottom so that gold, which is heavier than most other minerals, is trapped as water washes through gravel shoveled in by the miner at the top of the box. Many, including Horace Tabor, tried their luck, but found that the placers contained black sticky sand difficult to separate from gold without mercury. About the same time, Abe Lee, higher up the Arkansas Valley, lifted a gold pan from an icy stream and yelled "O, My God . . . I've got all California in this here pan."[107] Within a year 5,000 arrived at Oro City near the head of California Gulch.[108] California Gulch placers produced for a time and then declined. An estimated $2,000,000 was panned from the streams and rivers of California and nearby gulches.

Oro City had nearly become a ghost town in 1866. Most miners moved on, cursing the black sands that resisted releasing gold particles. One saloon owner tore down his building and panned thousands of dollars of gold from below the floor before leaving. In 1868, the Printer Boy Mine started producing well and set off a small rush that revived mining. [109] Except for some increase in hard rock silver and gold placer mining there was no boom.

In the mid-1870s William Stevens and Alvinus Wood dug a twelve-mile ditch from the Arkansas River for hydraulic mining of their placer claims. Heavy black sands continued to clog their sluices making separating the gold particles almost impossible. Suspecting a lead-silver ore they sent samples for assay. The results showed lead carbonate ore at twenty to forty dollars per ton. Telling no one, they quietly staked claims over nearly all of Rock and Iron Hills.[110] Their secret eventually got out and a new rush was on, but this time for silver. While the rush was at its peak, two prospectors working under a grubstake agreement for Horace Tabor, found the Little Pittsburgh. The Little Pittsburgh started the greatest legendary figure in Colorado history down the road to wealth, scandal of divorce and marriage to Baby Doe. The story ended with both in poverty.

During the boom days, the most direct route to Leadville from Denver crossed avalanche-prone Mosquito Pass from South Park. Even in summer, this route required toughness as one traveler described:

> *. . .The road over Mosquito Pass from the end of the track begin to look like the route of a demoralized army; there was no road — there were wheel-ploughed tracks upon tracks and sloughs of mud, dead horses and cattle by hundreds, scattered along wherever they dropped, and human wreckage in proportion . . . .*[111]

All winter, Mosquito Pass was windswept and snowy. Anyone crossing the 13,280-foot pass in winter or spring risked avalanche death. Travelers and mail carriers ventured over Mosquito Pass risking deep snow and avalanches that could bury a person without warning under tons of snow. The London Mine near the summit struggled with avalanches that more than once leveled its buildings. Avalanches ripped away telephone poles in the winter of 1899 severing Leadville's communication to the outside world. The poles were placed closer together, believing that this would give strength to the lines, but avalanches still carried away the poles like matchsticks. Burying the lines finally solved this problem.[112]

During the boom days in 1879, M. C. Barker and Patrick McQuillian took supplies to Spencer's mine near Mosquito Pass. Returning late at night the men reached Mosquito Creek's south fork when a sudden and severe storm overtook them. They were caught:

> *. . . in a lonely isolated mountain pass in a blinding driving fall of swirling snow [which] means little short of death and the chances for escape almost as slender as that of drawing the capital prize in a lottery . . .* [113] *unless shelter could be found.*

In panic the men attempted to head down the road at double speed. One mule suddenly balked and refused to move. Shouting, pulling and application of other forms of force could not coax the headstrong mule forward. The storm grew worse reaching white-out conditions with cold, wind, and moisture creating an even more dangerous situation. With the mule standing fast and the road lost to sight in the whiteout the men scuffed the ground for any stick that would serve to build a fire. Being above timberline, no firewood was found. Then they heard a dull crashing sound. Fear gripped them, as they knew the unmistakable sound of an avalanche loosening itself from the mountainside. At that point:

> *. . . a dense cloud of dust and snow gathered and arose, and when it cleared away Mr. Barker and his companion were appalled at the sight of the great snowslide rushing down upon them bearing on its bosom trunks of trees, large boulders, and a mountain of loose stones. The field was at least four acres in extent and about fifteen feet high, presenting an almost perpendicular front. Escape was out of the question . . . Both men turned to flee, but the cyclone of the mountains caught up and bore them down in an instant, and then away like a cork in receding breakers.*[114]

Barker lost consciousness for a short time, but snow melting around his face restored him to his senses. McQuillian was less fortunate and the object of the avalanche's wrath. He was hit hard to the ground and struck by a limb that caused him great pain. Barker could hear his screams as they were pulled along at the speed of a hurricane to the edge of a deep canyon where death certainly waited. Just as the edge of the avalanche reached the canyon the vast field of snow split, with half of it flying over the cliff making a boom-like artillery, but the portion carrying the men careened from right to left and back again until finally slowing and coming to a stop in a small creek. Both men ended their ride on the surface and they immediately began struggling to free themselves, but more snow came in the wake of the slide and buried them.

The avalanche buried Barker to his armpits. After tremendous effort he managed to dig out of the nearly rock-hard snow. Hurriedly he started searching for McQuillian. A large pine bough sticking out of the debris attracted his attention. On a hunch he started digging for McQuillian. For two long hours he dug and eventually found his partner, badly injured, but alive. The bough that first caused McQuillian pain created a small cavern around him providing protection from being crushed and trapping an ample air supply for his survival. McQuillian avoided the most common cause of avalanche death — asphyxiation.

Barker had a painful sprained ankle and contusions, but managed to assist his semi-conscious friend to a nearby ranchhouse along the road to Alma. The rancher helped with their wounds and provided them food while they rested.

The next day Barker returned to the avalanche, expecting to see the team and wagon destroyed. Instead, he found the team grazing and the wagon safe and whole. The mule had sensed the danger and had stopped in a safe place. [115]

Stories like these had little effect on wealth seekers as strikes at Leadville brought thousands to the two-mile high city. Silver and gold with their promise of an easy life called stampeders to flock to Leadville and the peaks all around. Leadville swelled to a population second only to Denver's. Prospectors fanned out into the hills and gulches looking for the one lode that would bring them great wealth. Already just a few miles northwest on Homestake Mountain, the first profitable silver mine in the Leadville district was in operation. Homestake Mountain is an isolated peak with its pyramid-shaped summit jutting high at the north end of Sawatch Range. Homestake Mountain can be plainly viewed from Leadville. The mine began producing silver during gold rush days in the 1860s. Prospectors generally overlooked silver deposits for the glitter of gold, but some miners could not ignore this lode of silver on Homestake. It was mined for a few years in the 1860s and 1870s. In fact, the first smelter in the district at Malta was constructed to process ore from the Homestake.

The Homestake was the oldest silver and lead producing mine in Lake County.[116] It was discovered by W. A. Crawford and two others trying to find a route over Homestake Peak. The ore assayed at thirty percent to sixty percent lead and 200 to 500 ounces of silver per ton with a trace of gold.[117] At the time of discovery this first silver mine in the Leadville region had no local smelter, so the ore was shipped over Mosquito Pass to Alma. Production increased to the point that August R. Meyer built a smelter at Malta at the head of California Gulch. The early owners of Homestake were McFadden, Smith, and others and the mine was worked extensively with drifts and shafts until the water level reached a point that it became necessary to drive a long drainage tunnel. With production restored Homestake continued producing until the new tunnel was stoped out. Then in 1878-1879 the silver rush began and the mine was temporarily abandoned while miners looked for their own strikes. After the boom settled various parties worked the mine with some success.[118] A small town called Lake City grew up near the Homestake Mine at the head of the west branch of the Arkansas River at an altitude of 11,550 feet west of Tennessee Pass.[119] At one point a community of forty cabins and several businesses existed. Avalanche threat and transportation difficulty eventually caused the town's demise. In 1881 a slide killed four men in their cabin, and in 1885, ten died in the same area. Eventually avalanches completely obliterated the town, but traces of foundations can still be found.[120]

The boom that made Leadville the silver capital of the world came in the late 1870s. Hundreds seeking wealth arrived in Leadville every week to be at the focus of the West's silver bonanza. Newly rich silver barons drove expensive carriages along pedestrian-crowded streets while dodging heavy ore wagons hitched to long mule teams on the way from the mines to the smelters. Swarms of people rushed along plank sidewalks and crossed muddy streets to homes and businesses. Utility poles lined the streets, carrying electrical and telephone services to Leadville, one of the first cities in the country to have such conveniences. Unnoticed, two miners rode into this chaotic and crowded scene.

These miners had just come from Homestake Mountain. They told of a horrible discovery. Their tale reminded people that just a short distance away there existed the remoteness and danger of the wilderness.

While prospecting on Homestake Mountain the miners had found a cabin that contained two dead people. Evidence indicated that an avalanche had caused the disaster. They had died of asphyxiation since the cabin remained intact with the roof caved in, but not crushed to the floor. The bodies sat posed in the same life-like position as before death so quickly struck. Their bodies were frozen and so looked recently deceased. Years earlier, about 1860, these souls left their loved ones to search this far off mountainside with hopes of finding a better life. Their names were never discovered and their fate never known by those they left behind.

The mining age brought forth anticipation as no other time. An average person, for the first time in history, could obtain fantastic wealth through means other than inheritance or through marriage. Many came seeking a grubstake where a merchant would provide supplies to a prospector for a percentage of the find. Many came and tried their luck in the gulches and hills supported by meager savings or money from home. Others wanted to start a business, or work for higher than average wages that were paid in boomtowns. Whatever the means of support one fact could be applied to every stampeder; all were motivated by the desire for great wealth.

To this scene came young Albert Morrison. He sought better wages than could be earned farming in New England where he grew up. Albert desired to pay off the farm mortgage that burdened his family after his father's early death. He planned to save a little extra money and return to marry his girlfriend Charlotte who patiently waited for him. Good fortune was his when he landed a coveted job at Leadville's post office. Albert and Postmaster Joshua Watson became close friends. Steadily he earned money to pay the farm mortgage and still manage to live in the expensive town of Leadville. Every day he observed tenderfoots pouring into town anticipating a life of ease. Equal numbers left for home no better off than when they first arrived. Albert slowly accumulated his nest egg and looked forward to the day he would return to his mother, the farm, and Charlotte.

Albert could not avoid looking out from his workstation and seeing the beautiful carriages of newly-rich people roll by on the way to some great event. Such sights reminded Albert of the rewards that finding a rich lode would bring. A life without worry could be his and for those he loved. As long working hours consumed his life for six days a week Albert determined to find his Eldorado. He knew quick wealth was an aberration, but it did happen. A case in point was Horace Tabor who became a millionaire after twenty years of chasing the dream. For a time Albert resisted temptations to prospect, invest, or grubstake others in their searches. His resistance finally faded when a miner friend, Jack Carroll, told him a tale of a lost mine.

Jack told Albert about an old Cornish miner who spoke of a rich mine on Homestake Mountain as he lay dying. The company that owned the mine employed the old Cornish miner. One day, the Cornishman discovered a rich silver vein, and reported it to his supervisor as he assumed any good employee should do. Expecting congratulations, even a raise, he instead received his pay and dismissal at shift's end. This puzzled the Cornishman who knew very little about American mining laws. Back home in Cornwall, the mining company owned mines outright. An individual could not make private claims on any discovery. If a miner found a new lode on company property a report to his supervisor would probably lead to a raise or bonus. In America, companies usually leased mines. The mining company had no rights to any new discoveries beyond the lease period. This created a different situation. If an individual found a rich vein he might hide the discovery, wait until the lease expired, and acquire it by a winning bid. In the Cornish miner's case his supervisor wanted a chance to bid on the lease and dismissed the miner to keep it quiet. With his last breath the Cornishman described to Carroll the mine's location — at least to the best of his recollection. He was unsure if the vein had ever been exploited. The Cornishman described the ore as rich in chlorides and containing great clusters of silver wire. He said that the Spanish before the arrival of the Americans had worked the mine. All his descriptions pointed to Homestake Mountain, and the old miner believed the vein might still be untapped. Then his life slipped away. Albert agreed to join Jack Carroll in this mining adventure.

On Christmas Eve in 1881, Albert was writing the letter that informed his mother of the changes in his life. He was attempting to console and comfort her and to allay her fears of mining. Assuring her that he was safe and comfortable he went on to tell his mother of the venture. Albert described the mine as a "hoodoo" that had impoverished everyone who owned the lease. For this reason, no loans could be secured, so Jack and Albert needed partners. They hooked up with two experienced miners, Hugh Temple and George Summers. The foursome pooled their resources, bought supplies, and settled in at a cabin on the mining site just as winter fell over the barren peaks around Leadville. They prepared the cabin against intense cold and the Sawatch Range's deep winter snows. Spaces between logs were chinked with mud against the weather. Spruce logs were chopped and stacked close by to keep a crackling fireplace going. For insulation they

piled dirt against outside walls to the bottom of the windows. With supplies laid in, the cabin repaired, and enough fuel for a long season, the
entrepreneurs began opening the mine entrance. The mine itself consisted of an adit 400 feet long and a shaft about 160 feet deep. The timbers had rotted away with debris covering and blocking the adit in
places. The shaft was half-filled with debris and cave-in material. The
tunnel was cleared and work continued to find the hidden vein.

As midnight on Christmas Eve approached, the men were comfortable in their one-room cabin. After a day working, Jack Carroll slept
soundly in his bunk. Summers and Temple played cards in front of a
dancing fireplace. Albert sat at the table writing a letter by a hurricane
lamp's light explaining to his worried mother why he chose the risky
and dangerous mining profession. Outside snow fell heavily as it had
for several days. As midnight approached, Albert decided to turn in for
the night. He wrote, " . . . this letter is not half-finished, but an old clock
there on our improvised cupboard is about to strike twelve, so for
tonight I will content myself with wishing you, dearest mother and
Charlotte . . ." Before he could write the words "Merry Christmas"
Albert died.

Moments before, a huge mass covering several acres broke loose
from its precarious hold on the barren tundra slopes far above the
cabin. Gathering tons of snow the avalanche hesitated for a moment,
but soon gained speed. Collecting more mass and speed, a billowing
snow cloud burst at least a hundred or more feet into the air and out
in front of the main body. The slide reached a speed of at least 100
miles an hour. The avalanche moved so fast that air was pushed aside
creating a vacuum. As it rode over the cabin roof the vacuum sucked
out all life-sustaining oxygen killing Jack Carroll, Albert Morrison,
Hugh Temple, and George Summers.

The New Year arrived and passed. One day, Postmaster Joshua
Watson walked by Albert's post office box and noticed that letters completely filled it. Joshua and Albert had made an agreement that once a
month Albert or a partner would come to town, pick up the mail, and
check in with Joshua. Joshua pulled the mail from Albert's box and
checked the postmarks. Uneasiness set in, then shock, as he read dates
that were three months old. Anxiously, he looked for one of his mail
carriers who knew the area where the fellows worked. That evening
the carrier set out on skis. Twenty-four hours later he returned.
Silently the carrier removed the leather straps that bound his boots to
the skis. Watson was horrified, suspecting the foursome was probably
dead. After a time, the carrier managed to tell Watson what he found.
The mine tunnel and cabin lay beneath a giant avalanche. No signs of
life could be detected. It looked as if the slide had occurred many
weeks before.

Watson later wrote an account of events to Albert's mother. He told her that when Leadville experienced disasters requiring military-like organization General Cook took charge. Watson continued, that on the next morning after he learned of Albert's fate, fifty men, with sleds, picks, shovels, and poles skied or snowshoed through the pine outskirts of Leadville on their way to Homestake Mountain. They arrived before noon, all set to pick and shovel a shaft through the avalanche. They struck the heavy timbered roof and after a few more hours uncovered a window. Breaking it, they entered the dark, musty cabin. Lanterns were passed inside, illuminating the place with an eerie flicker. Summers and Temple sat by an ice-cold fireplace with playing cards still in hand. Jack Carroll lay on his bunk as if only asleep. At a table young Albert hunched over the letter, still in mid-sentence, from the night before Christmas, a few weeks earlier. Postmaster Watson wrote to Albert's mother that:

> . . . *loving hands tenderly raised the remains of the boys to the surface and laboriously brought them to the city on sleds that they had provided, followed by as sorrowful a conclave as ever entered the gates. After lying in state for thirty-six hours they were buried* . . .

Joshua sent Albert's unfinished letter to his mother. In his letter Albert described the fever for wealth that infected hosts of people coming to Colorado, where people could pan streets for gold dust which fell from pockets of the many men who walked or rode through the busy and crowded city. He explained how he fell under the spell of attaining enough money to raise his mother, his future bride, and himself above a subsistence life. In this writing, his last letter, Albert continued to reassure his mother and Charlotte:

> . . . *Thus far this winter has been an exception. Little difficulty was experienced by us when three weeks ago we came over with our provisions, in picking our way thro [sic] the pines and chaparral . . . or in rolling up the sides of the mountain with our pack animals. We may be favored with a communication of mild weather for some weeks yet. Although we have been governed by the experience of others in time past and brought sufficient food to last three or four months. There is plenty of wood and abundance of water on the claims, and we shall not, in any contingency, suffer from anything except the possible isolation I have referred to. To be without letters from home or the daily newspapers for weeks at a time, when the lights of a large city are to be seen*

from your cabin windows, would indeed be a painful anomaly, and I am told it is very likely to happen. Should it occur, you may be a long time without advice; but you will be comforted with the assurance that your boy is very well provided with a warm cabin, suitable clothing, agreeable companionship and reading matter in abundance.[121]

Besides sending Albert's last letter, Joshua Watson went on to share with Albert's mother about the proceedings upon finding his remains:

. . . it is with a heart filled with grief that I essay a reply, for your boy was to me all that another not of my own blood well could be. On the day you wrote the anxious letter before me we laid him away in Evergreen cemetery, side by side with his companions, their remains having been followed to their last resting place by the largest concourse of people ever gathered for a like purpose in this city of sympathetic hearts. Already money is being subscribed for a suitable monument for their memory, and this it is intended shall be ready for unveiling on the next decoration day. Lest the newspaper containing an account of the calamity that overwhelmed them shall not reach you, I will undertake to briefly to give you the painful facts . . .[122]

Joshua wanted to console Albert's mother and Charlotte with the comfort of knowing his last life moments were spent thinking of them.

. . . He had been engaged in writing a letter to you, and when the awful shock came his hand, still holding the pen (this I am sending to you in the mail) with the point on the final letter "e" of the word 'Charlotte' . . . It is enough to know that death was instantaneous and necessarily painless. "
Joshua ends his letter, " . . . If words could still the anguish of your heart at this moment, dearest madam, be assured I should not spare them. It seems to me, as I write, the tenderest, humanist thing I can do is to leave you alone with your holy grief, and command you to the Mother of Sorrows for Consolation.
Joshua Watson
Postmaster[123]

An avalanche catastrophe in the same area overshadowed this tragedy only four years later causing Colorado's first large mining disaster.

In the winter of 1884-1885, a workforce of ten miners stayed at Homestake Mine. Well supplied and mostly snowed in, the men had not visited Leadville for some time. In mid-February, Horace Mathews penned a letter to his cousin Bessie. "Snow, snow, snow! Will it ever stop?" The letter was dated February 21, 1885. The other nine men rested, played cards, and contented themselves in various ways, as a storm raged outside. For two weeks a storm pounded Homestake Mountain and made the mine entrance inaccessible, and all work stopped. Horace and his co-workers waited for a break in the storm.

Each man had a different background from the others and a unique reason for coming to this remote silver mine. Marton Borden, his brother Sylvester, and Englishman Thomas Burt were miners by profession. John Locke, the "limey," as the others referred to him for his English birth, owned a cattle ranch near Denver but dreamed of wealth from silver. Jim Burns from San Francisco came for adventure and dreams of a life of leisure. Horace and his brother Joseph Mathews wanted to try mining for its possibilities of sudden wealth. Charles Richards, Chris Harvey and Robert Campbell became convinced of the value of the mine and chose to invest their time and money.[124]

Overhead the men heard roof timbers creak under the weight of snow. Snowfall on the level reached the cabin eaves making it impossible to see out of any window.[125] Tunnels shoveled through deep snow connected the cookhouse and shed. Horace wrote that this "country is so cold and snowy that the canary is kept inside."[126] It was a reference to the bird miners carried to detect lack of oxygen. Canaries will die even before the miners' candles flicker out.

Undetected by the mortals inside, snow on the mountain above had accumulated over previous days to the breaking point. A sudden windblast cut the top snow layer high above the cabin:

> *The . . . sound of a rumble . . . slowly grew louder, reached a climax and then gradually died out. . . . Then, without warning, the room was filled with a roar . . . The roar grew louder. The rafters shrieked . . . a beam shattered with a cannon-like report . . . as a curtain of white dropped from the ceiling.*[127]

Several weeks later two friends, Martin Sweeney and Mike Conerty, stopped at the post office to pick up the mail and take it to the Homestake miners. Somewhat alarmed by how much had accumulated, they placed the mail in packs and started immediately for Homestake. When they arrived, Martin and Mike found:

> *. . . the gulch where the three cabins once stood filled with snow and every indication of an avalanche. The tunnel to the mine and the ore dump were covered with the snow.*

Rescuers at the Homestake avalanche disaster reach the top of the cabin and prepare to enter the building where ten miners perished in 1885. (Denver Public Library, Western History Department)

The men fired their pistols and made outcries, but only the echo came back . . .[128]

Where three buildings once stood none could be seen. Martin and Mike knew the truth though they held out hope that their friends had somehow survived. Silently the comrades skied to Frank Sanderson's Eight Mile House Ranch near Tennessee Pass.

Sanderson heard their story and determined to go and see if any survivors could be found. The next day April 25, two months after Horace Mathews penned his letter, Sanderson and ranchhand Ted Smith went to the Homestake Mine. Five hours later they returned and confirmed the unfortunate fact. Frank Sanderson sent news to Leadville's Sheriff.[129] The dispatch came to Denver City Mine foreman, James Murray, in Leadville stating that " . . . the men at the Homestake have been buried in a snowslide. Send relief."[130]

Several lines of men on skis prepare to shove off with some of the victims of the 1885 Homestake disaster that killed ten miners. It was the worst mining disaster in Colorado's history up to that date. (Denver Public Library, Western History Department)

They posted and circulated the telegraph. Nearly a hundred volunteers quickly assembled. The Denver and Rio Grande Railroad provided a special train for carrying rescuers to the staging area at Sanderson's Ranch on the Eagle River, seventeen miles from Leadville. Sixty searchers with necessary tools boarded the special train for Sanderson's Ranch.

Upon arrival, Sanderson told volunteers the snow lay too soft and deep to make adequate progress, so they waited and set out for the catastrophic scene the next morning. Overnight the snowpack settled and hardened. At first light the search party started the long climb to Homestake Mine on skis, arriving about eight in the morning. George W. Cook, Leadville's experienced disaster relief leader and organizer, took command of operations as he had four years earlier at the 1881 Homestake avalanche.[131]

Hauling Homestake avalanche victims to the Sanderson's Ranch where a Rio Grande train waits to remove the bodies to Leadville. (Denver Public Library, Western History Department)

Freshly-fallen snowcover temporarily obscured the terrible sight from these Good Samaritans. They cleared away the loose snow and found the avalanche surface hard as a rock. Using axes, picks and shovels they hacked and cut for several hours through forty feet of snow. The excavation commenced in three parallel trenches until finally they found the storehouse. From that point the searchers figured out the direction to the bunkhouse.[132] After digging for hours, they reached the rooftop of the nearly flattened building. Several burly gents removed a timber and entered. Inside a body could be seen. Though frozen the body showed no signs of visible injuries. One man lay crushed under several beams. Across the bunkhouse, three mortals embraced each other in a frightful pose clearly showing they survived only to freeze or suffocate. The limbs of the unfortunates were so strongly interlocked that six men struggled for half an hour to separate the men. Rescuers saw another man kneeling in prayer. Two others remained in their bunks apparently never awaking from sleep. Searchers explored and found two more killed by debris. All ten miners had died.[133] Volunteers sighted the first body at one o'clock in the afternoon, the last at nine p.m. that night. Heavy snowfall began so a retreat to Sanderson's Ranch seemed prudent.

While at the site a Police Gazette dated February 14, and a personal letter dated February 10 were found and Horace Mathew's letter was dated February 21. An alarm clock, frozen in time, showed 3:30. Still set to go off at 6:30 a.m., the clock suggested the slide occurred at night.

Monument to the ten miners killed at the Homestake Mine in 1885. There were only eight markers as two of the victims were returned to their families. (J. W. Jenkins Photo)

Two days later, fifty rescuers pulling makeshift sleds returned. They placed bodies in canvas tarps secured by rope to the sleds. One by one they pulled the unfortunate miners to a waiting train for transport into Leadville. Upon arrival the bodies were removed to a morgue on Harrison Avenue. Leadville prepared for one of the unhappiest days in its history. It was the biggest disaster to visit a mine in the twenty-six years of Territorial and State history.[134] Town leaders held a meeting with standing room only and passed a resolution allowing the community to spend funds on a procession and funeral. A citizens' committee provided for an undertaker, coffins, burial robes, and interment expenses in the Evergreen Cemetery. Another committee answered letters from friends and relatives. So much money was collected from merchants, citizens, and even brothels that all the funeral expenses were paid with enough left over to provide relief to each of the miners' families. The bodies of Christopher Harvey from Central City, and James Burns of San Francisco were sent to their families for burial. The eight other victims received a solemn ceremony and proper burial.[135] An estimated 10,000 mourners passed by to view the bodies on the Sunday of the funeral.[136]

On funeral day:

> *. . . The sun never appeared over Mount Sheridan with greater effulgence than that of this morning . . . The sky was clear and the few clouds that hung about the mountain peaks soon vanished and left the entire aerial field to Sol.*[137]

Yet on this day, looking northwest, black clouds shrouded Homestake Peak as if in mourning for the men taken from life on its scoured and glaciated slopes.

Various groups, including the Great Western Band, First Brigade Band, National Guard, the Grand Army, and other civic societies, organized ceremonies. Charles Richards was borne to the Catholic Church of the Sacred Heart where services commenced. A huge procession moved with open hearse to Evergreen Cemetery where he was committed to the earth. At noon, thousands gathered along Leadville's streets and joined in a farewell for the others. At one o'clock, black crepe-shrouded hearses rolled up to the morgue and pallbearers brought out casket after casket. Slowly and with great solemnity, a procession moved along streets and past businesses draped in black. Bands played funeral marches. Hundreds joined the procession as it passed each street. At Evergreen Cemetery four graves were prepared to receive two caskets each. After final words and eulogies, the bodies were lowered.[138] Diggers covered the graves and the mourning crowds returned home. For two days, death wrapped Leadville in sorrow. Businesses stayed closed and few people ventured onto usually energetic streets. An angel-topped monument placed in September 1886 at the graves commemorated the ten who lost their lives at Homestake Mine.

Homestake Mine produced for several more decades after the 1885 avalanche, but no one dared live there again. Avalanches over the years have erased most evidence of Lake City near Homestake Mine except for some foundations, mine debris and an occasional milled board lying on the ground.

CHAPTER 4

Winter of the Big Snow: 1898–1899

> *. . . The town was in a little valley. On all sides the big snow mountains shut it in. Massive snow slopes and rocky summits towering above seemed about to fall and crush it. They built the plank sidewalks along the street raised some two feet above the ground, like walks I had seen in seaside resorts. . . . the snow up in these regions was so heavy during eight or nine months of the year that it was necessary to shovel it off the roofs of all buildings or it would crush them. Then the snow was shoveled into the street, so that in the middle of winter the street consisted of a mound of snow fifteen feet high extending its entire length, shutting off all view across the street, ...*[139] Charles Fox Gardiner, *Doctor at Timberline.*

From the mid-1880s to the year of the "Big Snow" avalanches continued to take a toll on residents in mountain communities and travelers along trails and roads. In the gulches and valleys around Lake City in Hinsdale County of the San Juan region avalanches threatened and occasionally made good those threats. In February 1886, at the nearby town of White Cross, Postmaster Tim Clawson became alarmed for the safety of James Watts and John Search who worked at the Hope Mine. Clawson returned from his mine and expected to see the men in town on Friday evening. He became concerned for their safety when they didn't show up for the weekend. After checking the men's post office box he noticed that the men had not picked up their mail as usual during the week. Concerned for his own safety if traveling at night, and while avalanche danger remained high after the recent storm, Clawson waited until morning. At day's light he and J. C. Bothwell made the trip to the Hope Mine. They found the gulch filled by an avalanche for a distance of over a mile. The corner of Watts and Search's cabin stuck out at one side of the slide. By the time Clawson and Bothwell reached the cabin four other men had joined them to search for the miners. Working feverishly the men picked and shoveled away debris around the cabin and were reassured when they heard the bark of a dog inside. After digging a little farther they freed the dog, but found the lifeless body of Jim Watts. Watts was thrown across the room by the force of the avalanche. Digging a few more minutes, they revealed the body of John Search.

Clawson assessed the situation and concluded that the men knew that sleeping in the cabin was dangerous and had moved their beds into the tunnel. Apparently, they returned to the cabin to prepare dinner when the slide hit.

In late January the men had left their mine after almost being struck by three separate avalanches that ran near their workings.

Clawson had urged them to stay in White Cross for a few days, but the men went back only to die. Sleighs were brought in to remove the bodies to Lake City for services and burial.[140]

Avalanches took life and damaged property, but sometimes slides cleared mountainsides of brush, and scoured away overburden making it easy to spot valuable outcrops. Avalanche action helped reveal a paying lode, but could lead to the death of those extracting the ores. This may have been the case at Vermont Mine near Lake City in Hinsdale County with its buildings constructed in an avalanche path at the site of the tunnel near the outcropping avalanching had revealed. Apparently, mine owners believed that either nature would stop acting naturally, or buildings filled with people would withstand a "White Death" assault. This situation caused the death of one man in the boardinghouse at the time of a slide, and later two more who had at first survived.

In the winter of 1887 a storm deposited snow deep on mountainsides, and wind rearranged the pack into cornices along ridges. Some miners at the Vermont Mine became alarmed as avalanches began running naturally in the vicinity. Some left for the safety of town until the danger passed. Others remained and continued working the mine. The slide that killed came January 13, 1887. The miners who chose to wait out the storm in town worried that an avalanche might descend on the mine. Their worst fears were realized when word of the catastrophe reached town. The men quickly organized a rescue party and made their way toward the devastation. As the rescuers neared the mine they saw a gulch filled deep with rock-hard snow, broken trees, mangled brush, huge boulders, and a mountainside devoid of any snow. The snow slid to the valley floor carrying with it the boardinghouse. The building, with the men who remained at Vermont Mine, lay in a heap at the bottom of the gulch. Rescuers set to digging and quickly found John Strom alive, but badly injured. Patrick H. McEnany broke his neck and back indicating he died instantly. They found Henry Repath alive. After receiving medical care in Lake City he returned to search for other victims. His exertion later culminated in his death. John Strom also died a few days later from his injuries.[141]

Some mine owners recognized the danger posed to miners by avalanches long before the Vermont slide. While many owners attempted to build quarters and buildings in safe areas to protect life, some threw the dice and hoped for the best. Owners sometimes constructed buildings right in avalanche paths as in the case of the Vermont. Built directly on the avalanche path, this fallen building brought home to owners, miners and county officials the need to carefully consider building sites in mountain gulches and on mountainsides. After the Vermont avalanche, rules for locating buildings away from known slide paths were suggested, but no real legal relief was imposed to alleviate some danger to those living and working in these high remote areas.[142]

A year later in January 1888, two men of the Aspen Water Company, Fred Rall known as "Dutch Fred" and another employee went to cut ice away from Aspen's water supply flume. A slide fell in Castle Creek burying Rall. The other man realized what was happening and used the crowbar in his hand to slow and then stop his slide. They took Rall's body into Aspen.[143]

Ruins of Ruby Camp near Crested Butte from the avalanche that came down Ruby Mountain seen above. An unemployed burro stands just left of center at the bottom of the photo. (Denver Public Library, Western History Department)

At Ruby-Irwin near Crested Butte an avalanche hit one of the biggest producers, the Bullion King, killing four in Spring, 1891.[144] The slide descended from Ruby Peak in early afternoon. The superintendent's wife, Mrs. Ropell, Captain B. F. Smiley, a mining engineer, the boardinghouse keeper and her young son succumbed.

Two weeks later, three more slide victims remained missing near Jacob Straeder Mine, close to Crested Butte. It was unknown exactly when it came down. The avalanche appeared to be a hundred feet deep and a half-mile wide. Rescue seemed impossible, although people looked with no positive results.[145] A mail carrier serving this area had a similar fate.

North of Crested Butte at Pittsburgh, in Poverty Gulch, the Augusta Mine produced gold, silver, and lead well into the twentieth century. People reached isolated Pittsburgh by walking or pack train along a rugged route. Snow and avalanches limited development. The company built a tram from Augusta Mine to the valley floor, but avalanches destroyed it in spring. The mill serving Augusta Mine failed because winter ore shipments stopped. In winter everyone had to stay at the mine. Once a week someone risked avalanche death and skied to Crested Butte for mail.

At the Ames slide near Ophir, an avalanche in 1897 followed a path created by timber cutting for the Liberty Bell and the Terrible mines. In late morning Ed Gamble, his wife, and Alex Fredlund waited in the Ames Depot when they heard that unmistakable roar. Just then a rock and log-filled avalanche shot through the depot. The three inside managed to free themselves unhurt, but outside five railroad cars were carried into the canyon below.[146]

As the last days of a cold January wore on in 1899, a front containing heavy moisture stalled in Colorado. At first snow fell in small amounts but then increased steadily. Close behind the first storm a second front arrived. After that yet another storm stalled dropping heavy snowfall for several days and then continuing over a period of several weeks. No one had ever experienced what would follow. Over a period of six weeks freezing temperatures persisted and snow fell without a break. Telephone and telegraph lines sagged and then broke. Deep snow isolated towns. Trains stuck fast in drifts or hit cement-hard debris left by avalanches that passed over the tracks. Some trains remained snowbound even after efforts to free them were made by plows, blasting, or armies of men. Some trains remained stuck until the spring thaw released them from their frozen crypts. Starvation became imminent in many Colorado areas. People set off avalanches and were killed as they worked their way along high mountain passes. Some folks set out on horse or skis or in wagons or stages and were not seen again until spring revealed their snowy tombs. Several slides crashed down and caused wholesale destruction and death where none ran before — or since. These events took place everywhere in Colorado, from the northern ranges south to the snowy San Juans.[147]

Digging out at the Ophir Loop Station avalanche. (Colorado Railroad Museum Collection)

Snow began falling on January 25, 1899. Near whiteout conditions produced deep snow, and winds caused deep drifting over streets, roads, trails and railroads. Communication broke down all over Colorado and in the mountains. Railroaders usually anticipated difficulty in winter, especially along high mountain passes, but this storm was different. Four main railroads, the Rio Grande, the Rio Grande Southern, Denver, South Park and Pacific, and the Colorado Midland provided economic lifelines to towns and mining communities. All these mountain railroads experienced partial or complete closure from snowfall, drifts and avalanches. Engines, always equipped with wedge plows on the front in winter, could push light snow and moderate drifts aside as trains barreled along their steel roads, but this storm stopped the trains cold. The monster rotary snowplow could clear deep snow and avalanches if free of debris. The big snow brought debris-laden avalanches down everywhere along canyon routes and mountain passes. Men with muscles of iron shoveled drifts and avalanches, but these efforts met with defeat. Dynamite, the friend of the hard rock miner, came into use, but soon after clearing one slide another would rumble across the grade.

Reports over the state documented the severity of the weather. Since November, snow and cold already surpassed all records and by the last day of January this series of storms was being called the worst ever. Snowslides and drifts blocked roads and trains and at times the fate of a train, its passengers and freight was unknown. At Leadville, they reported it the worst snowstorm ever witnessed. At Silver Plume the drifts became so deep that many people became concerned for the safety of the town and area camps. Cripple Creek became isolated off and on with trains held at stations or stalled in drifts. The plains received the same pounding. The Blue River Branch of the South Park Line was blocked by a snowslide. A passenger train that left Denver for Leadville ten days before could not return and stayed at the yards in Leadville. Boreas Pass between Como and Breckenridge defied every effort to open the route. On Kenosha Pass snow fell hard and wind blew in drifts so quickly that as soon as a train plowed through, the track immediately became blocked again. A train with passengers and supplies bound for Kokomo left Dickey and was not heard from for days. A group of volunteers organized at Kokomo set out to find the train. They found it at a siding blocked by an avalanche on each end. Kokomo was on the verge of starvation as were others towns including Leadville.[148] West of Boulder, Ward remained snowed in for three months. It required two hundred men working three weeks to open the "whiplash route" of the Colorado and Northwestern, also known as the Switzerland Trail.[149] This all occurred in the first days of a storm that lasted from January 27 to mid-March, 1899.

People needed coal and food and depended on reliable train service. Railroads were the key to life and industry in the Rocky Mountain Empire. Blockages must be cleared immediately to avert freezing and starvation. No sane person thought the storm would threaten the life of communities. It was assumed the railroads would always manage to reopen within hours, or at most a day or two. Coal was diverted to heating homes. Mines everywhere in the state closed without coal to keep pumps working to drain mines. Mining ground to a halt at the big producers at Leadville, the Ibex and Resurrection mines. With mines closed, smelters shut down operations and all of this threw large numbers of men out of work depressing the economy. Ore couldn't be shipped out and supplies couldn't be brought in.[150] Snowfall continued into a sixth day when the *Leadville Herald Democrat* reported:

> . . . amidst constant snowfall the skies promised no relief
> and there was a fear that railroads would succumb to rapid
> snow accumulation in huge drifts against which the attacks
> of the snow plows seemed ineffectual.[151]

*A break in the storm in Leadville in 1899. Snow in the street drifted
fifteen feet high. Walking was the only transport as trains froze to
the track in their yards and roads were totally impassable.
(Colorado Mountain History Collection, Lake County Public Library)*

The Midland and the South Park railroads suffered the most eco-
nomically in this long storm period. The Midland Railroad closed first
over Hagerman Pass. Drifts and avalanches blocked the route over the
high line through Hagerman Tunnel. Along the high route, avalanches
trapped four freight trains. Rescue efforts to bring out the railroad
crews failed. Train crews remained stranded in a blockade of white.[152]
Both the Midland and the South Park were unable to run a train
through their entire route for three months.[153]

The long, wide, majestic South Park region viewed from Kenosha
Pass lay in a deep white mantle. Trains moved no farther than Webster,
at the eastern base of Kenosha Pass. To open the grade the Colorado
and Southern Railroad Company, which owned the South Park line,
employed armies of men, plows and explosives to battle the drifts. They

lost the battle. Eventually trains made it only to Grant a few miles east of Webster. Widely separated towns in South Park faced a complete communication breakdown from the rest of Colorado. Trains could not bring in food, supplies, or fuel. Fear settled across South Park. The little bit of information that did get out described an extremely heavy snowfall and snow drifting so high that cows walked over farmhouses. People skiing over Boreas Pass, named for the god of the north wind, stopped to rest on the telegraph pole crossbars.[154] Leadville, not yet totally closed to the outside, rallied to send relief. Organized snowshoe teams packed supplies to South Park communities and stranded train crews in an attempt to reopen the line.[155] The Spotswood Stage Company, its coaches and tack stored since the railroad made stage-coach transport obsolete, reopened the old wagon and stage service. Four-horse teams pulled coaches or sleds and broke through the snowy blockade that brought trains to a stop. This heroic effort averted star-vation in South Park, Breckenridge, and nearby communities.[156]

With hardly a break the storm continued, but on January 30, snow-fall suddenly stopped. Relief lasted only a matter of hours. Smelters in Central City, Idaho Springs, Breckenridge, and Leadville closed down and sent the men home since ore could not be shipped or fuel and sup-plies brought in. An avalanche came down Democrat Mountain near Silver Plume and closed the wagon road and blocked the railroad grade from Georgetown. The Colorado Central Railroad managed to get the track cleared the same day.[157] On the last day of January snowslides obstructed sections of the Rio Grande and completely shut down the Midland Railroad's operations. The weight of snow brought down tele-phone lines throughout Colorado. Avalanches carried off poles and wires. Finally, an avalanche on Tennessee Pass blocked the Rio Grande Railroad, and Leadville, too, became cut off from the rest of Colorado. On a Rio Grande stop at Malta, just four miles south of Leadville, sixty coal cars sat immobilized and unable to move in either direction. Concern for the outlying camps grew by the hour. Few could go in or out of some areas even on skis. To alleviate the danger, the railroads and town hired hundreds of workmen who had been idled by the snow-blocked roads and trams to mines and smelters. They cleared side-walks and rail yards of drifts, and chipped away ice that froze the railcar's steel wheels to the tracks. This storm deposited so much snow that people entered and exited second or third-story windows.[158]

The Rio Grande fared better than most mountain railroads. At least some sections remained in service, but they actually suffered more injuries and fatalities because crews, passengers, and equipment were placed in harm's way. On January 30, a Rio Grande train left Red Cliff for Leadville. An avalanche hit it and buried one man. He sustained only slight injury.[159] Over Tennessee Pass in a narrow canyon near Red

Crossing the street in Breckenridge was made easy by a system of snow tunnels. (Denver Public Library, Western History Department)

Cliff an eastbound double-header passenger train ran headlong into an avalanche in progress. The giant headlight on the first engine disappeared downslope toward the river. The avalanche demolished the cab. The crew didn't see the avalanche as the train approached when:

> . . . *more than a few feet in front suddenly a mass of snow twenty-five feet in height and probably one hundred in length was noticed within ten feet of the engine coming toward them with great velocity. [Engineer] Russ immediately saw the emergency and reversed but not until it had struck his engine and the one following. His fireman, Ruminger, when he saw the mass approaching, made an effort to escape and was in the effort of leaping when the mountain of snow caught him and hurled him with terrific force back in the tank, burying him in its depths, though not injuring him. . . . The sudden stoppage . . . caused the passengers to leave their seats . . .*[160]

The crew, with great toil, dug a path to the damaged engine. After they uncoupled it, the train's second engine was able to pull the train into Leadville. Upon arrival the railroad men saw " . . . a scene presented at the yards . . . one of which has never been witnessed in the history of the camp before. The snow was everywhere from three to five feet deep on the level . . ."[161] Snow buried cars and engines under drifts. Passengers quickly disembarked and made their way to warm meals and rooms in Leadville's numerous hotels. The travelers waited out the storm that raged into February.

February 2 brought more snowfall, drifts and avalanches that interfered with railroad traffic. The Midland and Rio Grande kept sections of its track open and occasionally forced a train down the entire length of their systems. The South Park line remained completely shut down. In the Leadville yards, ice six to eighteen inches thick wedged against wheels of rolling stock. Crews had to chip away at each wheel before the engine could move any cars. The Rio Grande Railroad managed to keep trains moving over the easy, and low, Tennessee Pass to the Western Slope.

Across the Continental Divide in Summit County slides barricaded the Rio Grande Railroad's Blue River Branch. Several snow crews tried to work, only to be defeated when avalanches rolled in over a newly-cleared section. Knowing the futility of further efforts, and facing starvation, the men on the crews tied themselves together to avoid becoming lost in a blizzard and skied from Klondike to Leadville for supplies.[162] In other areas an avalanche buried woodcutters close to Alicante as they made their way from Wheeler to Leadville, but all managed to dig out and survived.[163]

Even Glenwood Canyon was not spared. In the early afternoon on February 3, a slide descended on the Rio Grande track nine miles east of Glenwood Springs at Shoshone. The night before a passenger train traveling west rammed into a slide filled with timber and debris. The engineer saw it, but evasive action could not avert a collision. He yelled to the fireman and both jumped as the engine struck. Car after car telescoped into the one in front.[164] Fortunately, only the mail clerk and express messenger were hurt and only slightly. Passengers, while shaken, suffered no injuries. Rescuers brought them to Gypsum.

Denver Hotel in Breckenridge during the long blizzard of 1899. Some rooms were entered through the second-story window. (Denver Public Library, Western History Department)

Crews with hand tools and a crane mounted on a flatbed car came in to remove the wreckage. They hardly had time to organize the effort when a small slide came down and covered the track nearby. Using the wrecking crane, the crew prepared to pull the empty passenger cars from the avalanche. Without warning, another avalanche struck squarely on the crew. Three men shot through the air and landed mostly unharmed in the Eagle River. Others rode on top of the avalanche and were unharmed since the heavy wrecking crane slowed the force of the avalanche before it struck them. The slide buried the two engines trapping Fireman A. W. Shade. Fireman Shade suffered for two hours in the overturned engine before rescuers punched a hole in the snow and pulled him to safety. He sustained burns to his legs that were caught against the firebox and a dislocated hip. Tightly-packed snow in the caboose held Engineer R. C. Steele fast. He suffered burns from a stovepipe that fell on him. Engineer George Hackett received a head injury but escaped from his engine. Three died. They found Roadmaster John McMahon, John Dempsey and John Mulvahill near the riverbank covered by snow six feet deep.[165] Two days later, a slide pushed thirty-two men clearing track in Glenwood Canyon into the Colorado River. Luck was on their side. The men were injured, but they all escaped death.[166]

Everywhere in the Colorado Rockies slides took a heavy toll in property and life. The narrow gauge Rio Grande over Marshall Pass, one of the few remaining open routes to the Western Slope, closed as trains stuck fast in heavy drifts. Rotaries from the town of Sargent worked on opening the route.

The Rio Grande Railroad's Blue River Branch finally succumbed to avalanches and closed. Attempts to reopen this route began on February 21, in a desperate effort to relieve the near starvation conditions in communities along the route from Kokomo to Dillon. The avalanche-prone grade had knocked a rotary plow off in 1893 killing two of the seven crew members.[167] Near the same location an avalanche knocked one of the relief rotaries off in 1899. This time its crew survived the power of the mass overturning the heavy machine and the cars in tow.[168]

At the difficult high line of the Colorado Midland west of Leadville the railroad

> . . . continues its heroic efforts against the Storm King and the officials are straining every nerve and fiber in overcoming the elements. They have a force of over 300 men at work in the vicinity of Hagerman clearing away the drifts and cutting the snow banks, but the prevailing winds which abound in the vicinity considerably hampered their work.[169]

The winter of 1899 the Midland Railroad lost revenue from the lucrative ore and freight-hauling business that sustained it. The Midland directors rushed to purchase the Busk-Ivanhoe Tunnel that had been abandoned earlier due to the exorbitant use costs charged by the tunnel company. Busk-Ivanhoe was lower than the Hagerman Tunnel and wasn't as susceptible to snow closure. A deal was struck, but it was too late for the 1899 season. The Midland Railroad faced the immediate problem of how to serve its Aspen and other Western Slope customers until it could reopen the Hagerman Pass route. In an unusual concession in the cutthroat competition between railroads, the Rio Grande permitted the Midland to operate trains over its Tennessee Pass route.[170] This concession probably saved the Midland Railroad from bankruptcy.

The South Park Road suffered the most of the mountain railroads. While trying to open a route to Breckenridge over Boreas Pass, the crew damaged a rotary plow. The plow returned to Como for repair, which left Breckenridge isolated with only limited supplies arriving by ski or stage, and with no way to obtain coal.

The branch between Leadville, Climax, Kokomo, and Breckenridge also closed and no effort was undertaken to open it before the weather showed signs of clearing. Avalanches isolated Kokomo from mid-January until April's end. The Denver South Park and Pacific Railroad could not keep it open with avalanches running across the grade daily.[171] A slide near Kokomo came down Jacque Mountain and covered the Wichita Chief Tunnel to a depth of one hundred feet. Another slide followed and destroyed the ore house, engine room, and other buildings that were built of heavy log construction. Consternation abounded that another avalanche would destroy the town again as one did in 1880.[172]

When the snow kept trains from arriving or leaving Kokomo and Climax, one resident set out from Kokomo on Norwegian skis. Will Zenocker made it to Leadville and described the winter scene and hardship of his journey. Traveling at night to avoid snow blindness, he rested in the early part of each day. He set off small avalanches several times. Any one of them could have become large, burying him unseen until spring. At times he came across slides that were still settling after a long fast run from high peaks. Other times he heard one come down in a place he just passed. When he reached Fremont Pass at Climax, Will saw several South Park engines. The railroad had brought them up to clear the line, but these engines lay "dead," covered by drifting snow, their stacks barely visible. They remained stuck until the storms ended and the lines everywhere else had been cleared.

The people of Breckenridge faced starvation. A supervisor sent news from Como that a train would attempt to break the blockade over Boreas Pass. Citizens rallied and came out in droves to clear the South Park tracks at the Breckenridge depot. On Boreas Pass the train rammed through snow. The crew blasted and shoveled frozen blockades. It had been three weeks since a train last negotiated the nearly 12,000-foot-high pass. Stock animals at Breckenridge had consumed nearly all the grain reserves, including that for human consumption. Relief came just in time. The supplies relieved the immediate suffering, but Boreas Pass became blocked again, with no hope of reopening until the storm passed.[173] The train continued a slow and difficult journey to Dickey and Kokomo giving some relief to those locations.[174] Dickey was the last place reached by the train. An avalanche twenty-five feet deep and filled with logs and rocks covered the track and defied clearing.[175]

On the nineteenth day of the storm, on February 11, the line to Breckenridge, Dickey, and Como still remained closed, renewing fears of starvation. Ski teams were organized. In long lines they pulled toboggans loaded with food from Leadville. They tied themselves together, guaranteeing that no one would become lost in a drift or fall over a precipice, as they made their way to Kokomo and Breckenridge.[176] February 13 brought a break in the storm, and temperatures finally rose above freezing.[177]

The first train over Boreas Pass bringing lifesaving supplies to Breckenridge in the Year of the "Big Snow" — 1899. (Denver Public Library, Western History Department)

The Midland Railroad remained blocked on Hagerman Pass. The Rio Grande stalled in Glenwood Canyon. The South Park Railroad became snowbound at Jefferson.[178] Trains on the high line below Hagerman Pass at Busk, could not get through, because the rotary plow was damaged clearing avalanches. Toboggans, pulled by eight men each, left Leadville with parts and provisions. Only one team made it to Busk. The others floundered and turned back to Leadville.[179]

General George W. Cook who had organized the teams that recovered the bodies of the Homestake avalanche fourteen years earlier

First train into Breckenridge after weeks of blockage on Boreas Pass during the "Winter of the Big Snow" — 1899. (Denver Public Library, Western History Department)

organized an army of nearly a thousand men and cleared the tracks to Malta by hand. There, the sixty coal cars, which had been stranded since the first days of the storms nearly three weeks earlier, were freed. Other trains filled with provisions that had piled up at Malta brought lifesaving food and supplies into Leadville.[180] Then General Cook moved his army up the Midland Highline to clear the track as far as possible. Towns and camps along the route neared starvation and cattle were dying in large numbers. General Cook also intended to cut a new road from Leadville to Pando to relieve the suffering at that location.[181] In spite of the General's organizational skills and leadership Hagerman Pass remained closed. Over the next few days the temperatures were milder and only light snow fell. Passes yielded to the efforts of men and machines and from Tennessee south to Marshall and the San Juans and the towns got some relief. Then on February 21, a new storm arrived and began dumping heavy snow undoing all that had been accomplished toward opening the railroads.

A big rotary plow had been sent out to clear the Blue River Branch of the South Park Line and was engaged in this work when the new storm started. While working west of Kokomo to clear the road to Dillon, Breckenridge and the other starving camps, an avalanche struck and hit several cars being towed behind causing the rotary to be pulled off the track and tumble into the creek bed. No one died in this incident as the deep snow cushioned and slowed the rotary's fall and allowed the men time to position themselves for the ride. Behind the rotary was a crew of a hundred men sent to finish clearing the tracks after the rotary passed, and this became a concern of officials in Leadville since the cars full of provisions were lost. A train went immediately to their aid, but when it reached the spot where the rotary fell track damage caused by the earlier wreck was not noticed and the engine overturned, but with no loss of life. The crew tramped back to Leadville and acquired another train and a toboggan. This time when the men reached the accident site they loaded supplies on the toboggan and hauled it to the hungry men waiting down the track at the station of Birdseye seven miles east of Leadville. Officials of the Colorado and Southern indicated that no other effort would be made to open the line to Dillon until the storm subsided. The citizens of Breckenridge called a meeting to organize a force to clear the tracks to Como, but the railroad officials would not guarantee delivery of provisions until the storm ended.[182]

East of Dillon toward Webster Pass, the snow was also piled deep. People walked over houses. One man was ill and skiers transported him to Como on a sled through tremendous drifts and across avalanche debris to save him. These hearty skiers remarked that they preferred the long ski of ten to eighteen feet in length, since they could reach speeds of sixty miles an hour.[183]

In Summit County, above Montezuma and Sts. John, an avalanche destroyed the town of Rathbone. Rathbone, also called Argentine, at 13,000 feet had a tenuous life from its start when a charlatan promoter, "Commodore" Stephen Decatur Bross, founded it in the 1860s. The mine experienced a period of decline due to the adverse conditions, working at high altitude, and the harsh winters. In spite of these troubles, the Pennsylvania Mine produced and occasionally revived under various incarnations. Despite the dangerous location, the mine's owners rebuilt the buildings after the Year of the Big Snow.[184]

Northern Colorado fared a little better during the first rounds of storms and stage service kept towns supplied. The February 21 storm finally closed and isolated towns throughout Routt County. Steamboat Springs became totally isolated but was not facing starvation. Outlying camps off railroad routes were also in good shape. Snowshoe teams were organized to bring in supplies from railheads when conditions worsened. Stage service to Steamboat finally succumbed and communication ended to the outside world, but the townspeople never became seriously at risk of starvation or freezing.[185]

The mail must get through. Even in snow as deep as a second story window these mail carriers made their rounds during the year of the "Big Snow." (Denver Public Library, Western History Department)

People in the San Juans taunted the "northerners" for having so much difficulty in a storm that was average for the southern mountains. There snow and avalanche blockages were normal and this year's storms were hardly different. The Rio Grande between Antonito and Santa Fe closed. The Cumbres line between Chama and Jimtown lay under heavy snow and avalanches, closing the route. But the railroaders in the San Juans were used to such pounding in winter, and the Rio Grande had more snow removal equipment on hand than at other locations. The railroad suffered only the normal stoppages and delays experienced in any winter season.[186]

A surprising and happy story came out of the Sneffels district. Mrs. James Wright and her two children left Yankee Boy Mine on skis for Ouray. They glided easily over hard-crusted snowpack. As the day wore on the sun warmed the snow. By the time the three skiers reached the Revenue Mine at three p.m. the snow softened so much they were sinking into it, which greatly slowed their progress. Eventually, one of the boys sunk deep into the snow and floundered. Mrs. Wright came to her son's aid and quickly became submerged up to her neck. They squirmed and struggled, but the situation seemed hopeless. They screamed for help but no one heard their cries. After a long struggle, Mrs. Wright momentarily lost consciousness. Upon regaining consciousness she heard the ominous boom of an avalanche breaking its tenuous hold on the mountain above filling the family with horror. Waiting for their impending doom, she closed her eyes. The slide crashed by within ten feet of the immobilized family and carried off the surrounding snowpack. In an instant the three skiers stood unharmed on an island of bare ground. The Wrights continued their trip to Ouray without further incident.[187]

The winter of 1899 recorded the first time an avalanche took a life on Parry Peak, the southern shoulder of Mount Elbert, Colorado's highest mountain. It happened at the Gordon Mine high above Twin Lakes. Its tram house was a huge structure easily seen from Twin Lakes. The other buildings that supported the workings were hidden from view, including a five-stamp mill and a boardinghouse. In later years the Gordon Mine became the scene of several avalanche tragedies. During the storm of 1899 on February 1, William Manning met death in a massive avalanche. Manning was a cook at the mine located two miles up the gulch from Twin Lakes. The snowfall alarmed the mine owner and miners because it accumulated deeper on the flat and higher in drifts than they had ever seen. Fearing a devastating snowslide, all but Manning retreated to the safety of Twin Lakes. On Wednesday evening a resident of Twin Lakes:

> *. . . heard a rumbling noise and looking up the mountain . . . saw an immense snowslide coming down the hill. It was two miles long and over three miles wide and carried everything before it. They saw the cabin in its wake and the next instant it was engulfed in the rushing mass of snow, ice and rocks. The slide was the heaviest and fiercest ever seen in the section and lodged further down the hill than any slides in the past. For a time the watchers thought it was going to cover up the little town at the lakes, but it spent its force, lodging within a short distance of the wagon road at the town.*[188]

Many buildings still stand at Independence across the Continental Divide west of Twin Lakes. The town was founded at the base of several large avalanche runs but did not experience a disaster. Thirty residents were stranded in the "Big Snow" but did not leave for fear of being caught while traveling. The citizens of Aspen became concerned for Independence's safety. A relief team on skis reached Independence with food and basic supplies in time to avert freezing and starvation.[189]

At the next large drainage south of Twin Lakes the mining town of Winfield had continued to thrive after the silver crisis. Nestled high in the upper valley of Clear Creek twelve miles west of the Arkansas, Winfield was laid out below high peaks that included 14,000 foot La Plata Peak. In early March the Payne family celebrated young John's birthday. Other guests came to enjoy the party. No one heard the start of a giant slide before it made its appearance and covered a portion of the town. The avalanche hit the Payne hose along with nearby houses and pinned the family inside. Those in the other houses managed to escape unharmed. A massive search began to locate the Payne home. All were found relatively fast and survived except for young John Payne. After such a horrible experience, Winfield's residents planned and constructed some of the best safety precautions against avalanches anywhere in Colorado.[190]

In the valley of "hot water," or Tomichi as the Utes who came to bathe called it, snow played a role in creating a legend of rich discoveries both found and lost. Few whites penetrated to the headwaters of Tomichi Creek before the Leadville boom. One exception was the Boone Brothers. They found gold in a tributary and built a sluice to extract the metal. Ignoring signs of winter the brothers stayed too late. A blizzard ended their lives, but the legend of "Snowblind Gulch" remained. For years the location of the placer was sought but never found.[191] The "Snowblind Gulch" legend persisted from the early 1860s until the first strike along Tomichi Creek in 1878. Though important, the latter strike did not live up to the legend. However, enough rich lodes eventually were located to support the communities of White Pine, North Star, and Tomichi.[192]

Even in normal years, heavy snows closed the local roads and could isolate White Pine and Tomichi from communication and supplies for weeks at a time.[193] In March of 1899, heavy snow fell and strong winds blew creating drifts deeper than usual even for this region. Avalanches came down regularly near Tomichi every winter. Enough danger existed that residents erected log and rock barriers to deflect slides away from town and mine workings. Usually these structures served well and no serious accidents happened.[194]

In the early morning of March 2, 1899, at the Magna Charta boardinghouse, Mike Smith sat at his table cutting meat with a knife. Mrs. Alta Stout, nursing an illness, slept on her cot. In a nearby cabin Mr. and Mrs. D. W. Sweeney and young Perry kept comfortably warm as the blowing snow piled deeply all around. Walking up the road from White Pine, a mile and a half south, Bert Stitzer and a friend brought laundry to a woman in Tomichi. Without warning they heard and then saw a tremendous avalanche nearly cover the town. After the shock wore off the men sprang into action. Bert's friend hurried back to White Pine for help and Bert proceeded to the disaster scene. Tomichi consisted of several substantial buildings including a bank, post office, saloon, grocery store, and several residences. These buildings had been flattened under the mass. When the snow settled there was no indication of human habitation.[195] In some places snow had piled up two hundred feet deep. Soon rescuers arrived with picks, shovels, and explosives. Most of the residents survived by digging themselves out or were speedily found. Mike Smith survived, since the logs supporting his roof crashed down and lodged at an angle, preventing him from being crushed by tons of snow. Rescuers reached him after several hours when they heard him tapping on a table with his knife. Perry lived because his mother's protective arms cradled him from the avalanche, but she and his father died.

Tomichi became little more than a wide meadow. A booming town of 1500 residents was turned into a place where only the occasional outline of a building can be seen. The avalanche of 1899 obliterated a once productive city. No one ever lived there again.[196]

Around March 10 the long storm period subsided and seemed to end. The worst winter in Colorado's history passed into memory or so it seemed. Temperatures began to rise and greatly assisted in opening roads and rail lines, but the respite lasted only a matter of hours. Although the next round of snow turned out to be less severe the new snow added the last straw which caused more avalanches, more closures, and more danger. Kokomo citizens complained that the Rio Grande neglected them after they turned out to help clear the track.

Then after the first train arrived after two months of blockage it carried unneeded supplies like mining equipment and nails. When the railroad was asked to bring a train of food and necessary supplies the railroad refused saying other towns were in dire need. Soon after, the storm geared up to a blizzard closing off Kokomo again.[197]

While warming temperatures made clearing easier it also loosened cornices built up by wind action on mountain ridges and on slopes below. This brought about more sliding and these slides carried more rocks and trees requiring labor of armies of men to clear. Then on March 24, the pause in the weather experienced for a few days turned into a raging blizzard. Towns recently opened to rail and road traffic once again closed. Avalanches ran in Black and Glenwood canyons covering tracks and stopping trains. The slide in Glenwood Canyon came down near the same spot that killed three people two months earlier. Near Sapinero, west of Gunnison, where the narrow gauge Rio Grande entered Black Canyon a train ran into an avalanche before any evasive action could be taken by the engineer. The engineer and fireman both jumped and suffered only minor injuries, and none of the passengers were seriously injured by the sudden stop. The Rio Grande and Midland were closed west of Leadville but managed to keep lines open to the east.[198]

The rotary on Marshall Pass ran almost constantly trailed by trains to keep the road open between Salida and Gunnison. In Breckenridge a fine network of tunnels connected businesses together so the new storm hardly affected the town. The rotary on Boreas Pass made it to the snowsheds on the pass but broke the hood and required a return to Denver for repairs.[199]

After a siege of more than six weeks the storms finally ended and trains moved along their routes bringing lifesaving supplies. Coal began to arrive in quantities that provided for home heating and enough for smelters and mines to reopen. Men out of work for extended periods returned to their work and could earn the money to sustain their families.

While this was the worst snow year in Colorado, it was not the record year for avalanche fatalities. With transportation so difficult and mines closed most people stayed out of harm's way. In fact several avalanches did destroy property at mines that would normally have had large workforces on hand, but these suffered little or no loss of life. But the winter of the "Big Snow" brought one of the state's worst avalanche tragedies. Heavy snows occasionally visit areas of the Front Range where camps and towns exist high on mountainsides. Seldom was commerce affected for long periods of time nor were destructive avalanches produced. The year of the big snow changed this situation nearly stopping commerce for weeks and causing one of Colorado's largest avalanche disasters.

Signs of impending doom were everywhere. The series of storms began to take its toll causing several fatalities in separate and isolated areas. Reports came in from mines in outlying areas that slides had taken out or damaged mine buildings and trams. Slides fell in places where none had slid before. Mines closed and workers made their way to towns. Some men were nearly killed by slides en route. Then at Apex near Central City an avalanche visited the home of Mrs. William Rudolf and her two children on January 30.[200] Mrs. Rudolph and one boy died. The avalanche entombed six-year-old James for two hours before rescuers reached the boy. He lived. The event took place in full sight of his horrified father who was just a few hundred feet away.[201] This and other deaths brought the toll to at least eight during this heavy snow season.[202] Then as the long stormy period wore on, one of Colorado's worst avalanche disasters happened at Silver Plume west of Georgetown.

In years past avalanches threatened Silver Plume and the immediate vicinity several times. Located at the base of Brown and Sherman mountains, Silver Plume experienced the fourth deadliest Colorado avalanche during the record snowfall winter of 1899. Silver Plume is one and a half miles west of Georgetown and forty-five miles west of Denver. The town received its name from the formation of its silver deposits which prospectors likened to the plume of a flower. The first silver discoveries took place in the 1860s, with Silver Plume reaching a population of 2,000 by 1870. Avalanches threatened, and occasionally damaged, buildings at the large producers — Pelican Dives, Snowdrift, Terrible, and Seven-Thirty — but none had run all the way to the town.

On Sunday morning at about 8:45 on February 12, 1899, a low sun peeked through the clouds that hung thickly over the valley and high peaks. After several weeks of incessant snowfall, the citizens of Silver Plume awoke to what seemed to be a brighter day. Households were busy with their daily chores — bringing in wood and water, frying hearty meals of bacon, eggs, and biscuits in preparation for work, play, and church. The sun poured shining light over the mountain peaks with its rays streaking to the valley floor providing a sense of relief from the lingering storm's oppression. On Brown and Sherman mountains, which rose above the town's north end, wind-blown snow had drifted deep into gulches. Snowfall had reached the brim of large catchment basins. Unseen, high on peaks, great cornices formed which precariously hung and strained under their own weight. Suddenly the sky grew dark. It appeared that clouds had moved in and a new round of snowfall started. Then the sky cleared. Something unusual had happened. Though some folks had heard a muffled boom emanating to the north of town, most did not accept the possibility of an avalanche landing on Silver Plume.

An avalanche had started far above Silver Plume in a large basin. It was channeled and compressed into Cherokee Gulch. The snow already filling that gulch added more snow to the avalanche's energy. Simultaneously another slide began in Swallow Hen Gulch, and joined with the Cherokee Gulch slide. The second one carried away buildings of the Seven-Thirty mines. Together this magnified the snow's force giving it enough mass and speed to carry it all the way to the valley floor. On its destructive ride down, the avalanche passed through Corry City Gulch and carried off several buildings of the Pelican Dives Mine. The ore houses filled with $50,000 worth of ore waiting for shipment when the weather cleared became part of the debris-laden avalanche as it continued its destructive journey. Superintendent Robeson of the Pelican Dives Mine was standing outside the shaft house and saw the movement of the snow as the avalanche started high overhead. Paralyzed for a moment at the horror of what he witnessed he gathered his senses in time to run to a place of safety just as destruction hit the mine. Continuing on its journey the slide gathered more snow and debris of timber and rock, and then this monster dropped full force on Silver Plume's northwest end, home to a large community of Italian miners. In its wake the avalanche furrowed a path ten feet deep for a distance of two miles. Several cabins disappeared or were swept away along with many inhabitants inside. Because the air was surcharged with powdery snow, Cyrus Lyon realized it was not a new round of snowfall, but an avalanche. He ran through town raising the alarm. Great dread gripped residents because about fifty people lived where the avalanche fell.

An alarm went out to the communities up and down the valley. A thousand people hastily assembled with shovels, picks, and muscle power. Frantically they began to search for the unknown number of victims. Within minutes they recovered Antonio Migretto badly injured but alive. Soon after, Antonio Maleano and Giuseppe Corennio were found alive. The three men were taken to a shed where they received medical attention.

By probing with long steel rods and blind trenching, the rescuers hoped to find more life under the ruins. The active snow load in the gulches above made the work more dangerous. Piling up to a depth of 100 feet in places it could crash down and bury hundreds more. No one spoke of personal danger, but they knew that another slide could kill them all. They posted sentries with rifles higher on the hill. Shots fired would mean an avalanche was seen or heard. At least the searchers would have a few moments to run for cover. All worked diligently and hoped that Providence would show mercy to them and the unknown number of victims underneath. In places the debris was seventy-five feet deep and packed hard enough to walk on without leaving footprints. The first body recovered was Joe Londini. Wagons and teams could not cross the rough rubble-laden avalanche surface, so crudely built sleds transported bodies to waiting wagons. By the day's end, they bore Londini and six other bodies to the Knights of Pythias Hall. It served as a temporary morgue.

Searchers digging trenches looking for survivors of the Silver Plume avalanche in 1899. (Denver Public Library, Western History Department)

Among those found the first day were Mrs. Destafano and her two children. She tightly clasped one child in her arms and the other was found a short distance away. Her posture indicated she had noticed the avalanche and ran to gather her children in an attempt to reach safety. With her husband still missing, rescuers continued until they found the cabin. Inside the fire still blazed and the Sunday meal continued cooking. The chicken coop was found next and all the birds were alive and uninjured.[203] As nightfall came the search ended.

As work continued the following day, three more bodies were found, but at least two men were still missing. At night fell and work ended as temperatures fell below the high of fifteen degrees below zero. Some residents left their homes for safer localities as winds loaded gulches and new cornices formed on ridge tops threatening Silver Plume with more disasters.

At first light the searching resumed and within minutes they recovered more bodies. Of the thirteen people buried, three survived. The dead included: Dominick Destafano, his wife and two children; Joseph, Peter and John Tondini; Jerome Guananzi; John Bietto and Enrico Navaria.[204] Destafano's entire family perished. Dominic stepped out of his cabin just as the avalanche hit. His wife and two children died in the cabin, crushed by the weight of the snow.[205] They did not find Dominic's body until spring behind the school building that still stands in Silver Plume.[206]

Body of Joe Tordino being carried from the Silver Plume avalanche of 1899. (Denver Public Library, Western History Department)

With all of the residents except Dominic accounted for, and without hope of finding him alive, the little mining community settled down. Surely no other catastrophe could befall them. The storms resumed.

Being apprehensive of the new snowfall along with winds that caused drifting, the miners at the Seven-Thirty Mine attempted to return to the safety of town each evening. On the night of February 21, three miners decided to stay at the mine, as heavy snowfall and gale force winds made it dangerous to leave. Whiteout conditions raised fears of becoming lost. At four o'clock in the morning, February 22, an avalanche ran once again down Cherokee Gulch. It demolished buildings, including the engine and boiler house, blacksmith shop, ore house, office, barns and several cabins of the Seven-Thirty Mine. In a nearby cabin John Levers heard the blast and jumped from his cabin window just as the slide struck, but he survived unhurt. The slide picked up John's cabin and turned it around on its foundation. Peter Oleson survived when falling roof timbers lodged in a way that protected him from the snow. His companions — Benjamin Nelson, and John Anderson — died. The avalanche ran its course down Cherokee Gulch to Dunderburg Mine where an old hermit, Daniel Fitzpatrick, lost his life when the edge of the avalanche crushed his cabin. Fitzpatrick had built the cabin and lived there for thirty years. David Jones, superintendent of the Seven-Thirty Mine, was in his cabin at the mine but the slide only grazed its edge. He made a fast trip to Silver Plume and set off the fire alarm to notify the town of this latest disaster. Superintendent Robeson immediately organized a search party and they started the dangerous winding trip to the Seven-Thirty Mine. While making their way up to the mine one man was blown off the road, so severe was the wind that blew. Italian miners, having experienced so recent a tragedy themselves, turned out in droves.

Searchers combed the debris area, digging and probing for survivors. Peter Oleson related his experience trapped for hours under the white:

> *Anderson, Nelson and myself were sleeping above the ore house in one room but in different beds. We were all asleep when the slide struck the building, carrying it over the dump. I was pinned in between the roof of the house and timbers. I had my reason all the time and could hear the men walking over me and calling to me, but I could get no answer to them for over four hours, when some one happened to dig there and make a hole into our prison. Then a big crowd of men soon took me out and, save for being badly chilled through and scratched some, I am unhurt. Medical attendance was sent for and they soon revived me.*[207]

After finding Oleson, gale force winds created new avalanche dangers, so searchers descended to safety. The next day they recovered John Anderson's and Benjamin Nelson's bodies at the Seven-Thirty Mine, and later Daniel Fitzpatrick was found unconscious lower in Cherokee Gulch.[208] He later died of his injuries.

*Monument for the ten Italian miners killed in the 1899
Silver Plume avalanche. The obelisk is Gunnison granite
from the quarry that supplied stone for the state capitol.
(J. W. Jenkins Photo)*

Later that year in Silver Plume Cemetery, the town erected a monument of Gunnison Granite — from the same quarry that provided

stone for the state capitol — nineteen feet four inches in height, inscribed with names of the ten Italian miners killed.[209]

Inscription on the monument at Silver Plume for the ten Italian miners killed in the 1899 avalanche. (J. W. Jenkins Photo)

The Silver Plume slide ranks fourth in fatalities in Colorado after the 1884 Woodstock avalanche on the Denver South Park and Pacific Railroad, a slide at Shenandoah Mine near Silverton in 1906, and a slide at Liberty Bell Mine near Telluride in 1902.

A disaster such as came to Silver Plume resulted from unusual weather. While such a disaster could visit Silver Plume, or any mountain community again, the conditions of 1899 have not been reproduced.

A year later near Tincup in Taylor Park three miners of the Enterprise Mine failed to return to camp after their shift. A large force turned out to find the three missing men and a search commenced. Finally a snowslide was discovered with tracks going in but not out the other side. For two days the search went on before the bodies of Tom McDermitt, Ed Robinson, and Harry Wyse were discovered.[210]

The winter of the "Big Snow" passed, but three years later a series of avalanches at a mine near Telluride would produce the largest number of victims in one day.

CHAPTER 5

The Snowy San Juans and a
Day of Terror at Telluride

> *Snowslides about Telluride have always menaced life*
> *because of the steep mountainsides and the consequent*
> *fearful velocity with which snow, once loosened, drops into*
> *the gorges. Telluride itself lies in a cup with precipitous*
> *mountains rising sheer up on three sides to the height of*
> *many thousands of feet. The mines themselves are far up*
> *these mountains, some of them above timberline. To reach*
> *them one must ascend a narrow and tortuous trail. The*
> *grade is too near perpendicular even for a wagon road. Ore*
> *is carried by means of trams, some of them several miles in*
> *length.*[211] — The Denver Times, *March 1, 1902.*

The San Juan Mountains are the most avalanche-prone region in Colorado and rank high among avalanche regions on earth. Avalanches have challenged travelers and disrupted commerce ever since the first explorers, settlers and prospectors entered this spectacularly rugged landscape. Prospectors traveled along rocky pack trails and built rough wagon roads through areas that were dangerous from first snowfall to spring runoff. They laid out railroad routes along precipices where slides fell and covered the track. Into narrow gulches and steep mountains they pushed railroads. Here slides descend persistently during and immediately after winter storms. Even in 1878 people recognized the increased danger of slides during and after a storm. After three people died in separate accidents immediately after a storm a newspaper appealed to its readers by recommending no travel for two days after its passing to allow the snowpack a chance to stabilize.[212]

An unfortunate accident illustrates the danger of winter travel in the snowy San Juans:

> *. . . One winter, Billy Maher and his Italian partner were*
> *mining in the San Juans, the snow rose to the top of the*
> *cabin. It was so cold inside that the partners had to take*
> *their potatoes to bed to keep them from freezing. Billy Maher*
> *tried to thaw out his dynamite by heating it in the stove, but*
> *it blew up, blinding and mutilating him. His partner went*
> *down the mountain for help, but the relief party of four were*
> *killed on their way up the mountain. Billy also died.*[213]

In the San Juans people have won only temporary victories keeping travel routes open against snow and avalanches. Paths and trails passed by necessity into steep valleys and ascended high on lofty peaks and passes which exposed teams of horses and trains to danger nearly all year long in Colorado's most mineralized region.

The San Juan Mountains hold a special place in the minds and hearts of those who live or visit there. They are characteristically different from other Colorado ranges having a:

> . . . *different appearance from any of the northern Rockies, — a more precipitous, alpine and grandeur countenance, with sharp pinnacles, tremendous vertically walled chasms, and extensive forests of spruce clothing their lower declivities . . . but nowhere else can be found whole groups of mountains holding their heads up to fourteen thousand feet, and having great valleys almost at timber-line.* [214]

The San Juans have the highest snowfall of the Colorado Rocky Mountains making winters longer than in the northern mountains.

The San Juan Mountains are rugged, steep, and unforgiving. Roads, when they were possible to build, barely hung on steep mountainsides. Where roads were impossible to build, narrow paths were hacked out that were dangerous to man and pack animals alike. If no trail or road could be constructed then mine owners slung trams up steep mountainsides and over deep chasms to reach mining sites often located high above timberline. Buckets filled with ore usually entered a mill where the ore was concentrated to lower transportation costs to smelters. Since travel was so difficult, working miners often stayed in boardinghouses at mining sites. Distance from point to point was not great, but the difficulty of travel precluded returning to town after each shift ended. Even in normal years winter produced heavy snowfall with avalanche danger always present.

Otto Mears, a Russian immigrant, built toll roads and eventually railroads throughout the San Juans. Mears served the Union Army in the Civil War and then came to Colorado. He opened a store in Saguache and hauled produce from the San Luis Valley to Leadville. On one of these trips his wagon overturned on Poncha Pass and spilled his grain everywhere. Former Territorial Governor William Gilpin happened along on a tour of mining in southern counties and stopped to help and give advice. He urged Mears to apply for a charter to build toll roads. This Mears did and the original roads over Poncha and Marshall passes are his creations. When discoveries that had been made west of Saguache showed promise Mears began the road and railroad building empire that eventually brought him national fame. With partner Enos Hotchkiss, Mears began construction on a toll road venture from Saguache to the San Juan region. Eventually time would give Mears the accolade of "Pathfinder of the San Juans." Mears eventually built over 300 miles of roads. They included routes still used, including the "Million Dollar Highway," from Ouray to Silverton, the most avalanche-prone highway in the country. Mears also built short line railroads. His Rio Grande Southern encircled the San Juans connecting to the Denver and Rio Grande Railroad at Ridgway and Durango.[215]

The Rio Grande Southern Railroad had to deal with avalanches more than any other railway in Colorado. In fact, the Rio Grande Southern never made a profit owing to the high costs of snow and avalanche removal and damage to facilities, grade, and snowsheds. So common were avalanches along this route that the slide paths received names. North of Rico the Nigger Baby and Hope Cross slides stopped trains cold. In Burns Canyon the Burns slide would cover tracks and occasionally rip them from the railroad bed. Five separate snowslides plagued Ophir Loop from the steep slope of Yellow Mountain. These slides sometimes cut both levels of the loop hopelessly trapping trains in between.[216] Rio Grande Southern's greatest difficulties manifested between Ridgway and Rico, a section that included Dallas Divide.

Roads or railroads eased travel in the San Juans, but conveyances required special engineering to negotiate roadbed or railroad grade. Wagons and stages were outfitted with sleigh runners for downhill runs. When traveling down steep mountain roads anchors were dragged behind to slow heavily-laden ore wagons, or logs were set and tied to rear wheels so they could not turn.[217] Railroads needed plows permanently installed on the front of the engines and hired extra track-clearing crews adding tremendously to operating costs. These flange plows cleared small drifts and moderate snowfall as a train moved along the track. Wedge plows were mounted on a flatcar and pulled behind the engine to remove deeper drifts, and if the train traveled at high enough speed it could throw the white mass far from the grade. Rotary plows handled the deepest snowfall and drifts. As many as four engines pushed these plows and had a fifth engine turned around to pull the plow out if it became stuck. Plows failed if faced with heavily packed, debris-laden avalanches. To tackle this, a crew known as "snowbirds" cleared grade obstructions using mining techniques. Picks, shovels, and high explosives loosened avalanches making removal from grades possible. Despite hardships in building and maintaining railroads, iron pioneers using muscle and powder pushed steel roads deep into the San Juan ranges.

Wherever railroads penetrated the Colorado Rockies snow and avalanches caused constant problems. Railroads crossed high ranges and the Continental Divide barrier and were exposed to extreme avalanche danger. Often they came upon an avalanche still running or one just settling on the track and hit it before coming to a stop. The railroads paid a high price in lost property and sometimes lives. The Rio Grande Railroad sometimes had trouble in Glenwood Canyon at Shoshone. Colorado Midland Railroad, the first standard gauge railroad in the Colorado Rockies, faced heavy snowdrifts and avalanches over the Divide west of Leadville. It passed over the highest average range in the state, the Sawatch, under Hagerman Pass between Leadville and Aspen. The Midland's high line route through Hagerman Tunnel required some of western mountain railroad's most extensive snowsheds. Snow and avalanche removal became commonplace along this route as a rotary plow description in the *Aspen Democrat* tells.

> *The rotary snowplow is a machine of large proportions having the appearance of a 'sawed-off' locomotive. A mammoth wheel, resembling a water wheel revolves in the front of the machine. The wheel gathers up the snow and whirls it up through a large funnel on the left of the machine, throwing the snow far out of the course of the tracks. The engineer on the plow handles this wheel, who occupies a station in the cab directly behind the wheel. . . . While at work on the slide snow mass they encountered in the morning, some large rocks and timber damaged the wheel to some extent, but not enough to put it out of business.*[218]

A working rotary looks much like a modern snowblower, but on a huge scale.

Snowshed on the Denver and Rio Grande Western Railroad south of Silverton in Animas Canyon c. 1884. (Denver Public Library, Western History Department)

The Rio Grande Southern and the Denver and Rio Grande Railroads employed the largest fleet of rotaries. The Denver South Park and Pacific Railroad had a large number of machines for the troublesome routes over Boreas Pass and at the Alpine Tunnel from St. Elmo to Pitkin. It was in the San Juans that snow and avalanches created the most havoc for railroads. Most affected were the Rio Grande from Durango to Silverton and the Rio Grande Southern looping the ranges from Ouray to Telluride, Rico and Durango.

Chattanooga was located between Ouray and Silverton. Rich mines produced ore high in silver content that had to be shipped two hundred miles to smelters. Pack mules hauled ore from remote mines along precarious trails then transferred the valuable cargo to wagons. Otto Mears alleviated this limiting factor on production when he completed a toll road in 1884, followed by a railroad in 1888.[219] Throughout Chattanooga's history people worked in nearby mines. In 1888 an avalanche hit, but Chattanooga rebuilt and carried on. But, in the late 1890s another slide destroyed Chattanooga and residents decided they should abandon the town.[220]

High operating costs to keep trains moving and constant repairs to the railroad's grade and facilities spelled the demise of the San Juan mainline.

Thomas E. Walsh managed a pyritic smelter in Silverton in the 1890s. Up to that time few prospected for gold in the San Juan Mountains as silver was found in much more profitable abundance. When Walsh came to the San Juans he had already amassed a small fortune in hotel and mining businesses. Always searching for a paying mine Walsh scoured the hills. Prospectors had long ago given up the search for a gold bonanza, but a few like Walsh and Andy Richardson still searched the San Juans for a mother lode. Silver dominated San Juan mining and it was silver that provided the miners with a livelihood for several decades. In the nearly inaccessible San Juan Mountains miners could ship only the highest-grade ore. At mine sites they left millions of tons of tailings on hills and in the valleys. Walsh had an idea. Why not check old dumps and have the tailings assayed? They might be able to profitably reprocess these discarded materials since reduction techniques had improved over the years. Additionally, the mine itself might be reopened at a profit. Walsh hired Andy Richardson to sample tailings in Imogene Basin.

To their surprise, ore from the Gertrude Mine dump assayed at eighty ounces of gold per ton. Together the men went to the mine and attempted to enter its tunnel and take wall samples. An avalanche blocked the entrance. They tried, but could not dig their way inside. After warmer weather softened the snow Walsh returned and dug into the tunnel entrance. He took tellurium ore samples assaying at $3,000 a ton.

Quietly, he bought claims around the site and developed his holdings into one of the most valuable mining properties in the world — the Camp Bird.[221] The Camp Bird Mine produced for the next seven decades.

At 11,500 feet high in Imogene basin at the upper workings of Camp Bird, Andy Richardson and eight men lived in a cabin. In the winter of 1896-1897, an avalanche twenty feet wide and a mile long came down over their place burying the cook and two other men. A miner saw it hit and made an effective rescue.[222] This avalanche experience was only one among many at Camp Bird.

Camp Bird miners faced danger daily in winter and spring. The Camp Bird management went to great extremes to provide an environment of comfort and safety for the workforce. At the turn of the century the Camp Bird's boardinghouse had electricity, steam heat, sewage treatment, marble lavatories, and reading rooms, but its location was exposed to snowslides. They made plans for creating safer conditions. To avoid a disaster the Camp Bird Company solidly constructed a heavy timber boardinghouse, anchored it into the hillside, and topped it with a steeply pitched roof. The steep roof shed snowfall and an occasional snowslide harmlessly off and into the vast valley below. Many nights miners sat in repose reading a good book, or smoking a cigar after a fine meal provided by the company, and noticed the single lightbulb, suspended by a twisted electric cord from the ceiling, tremble and swing as a slide passed nearby. Even without slides heavy snowfall could build up to ten feet deep on the stout boardinghouse roof.[223]

On the Sneffels road, about 1900, the famous Ashenfelter freighting company lost a wagon train with several wagons, drivers and six horses per wagon at "Waterhole Slide." The Waterhole Slide is so named because of the practice of teamsters driving through the stream at this point so animals could drink after loading wagons with ore at the Camp Bird Mine. Only in summer did snow finally melt from the gulch revealing the wreckage of men, animals and ore wagons.[224] Close by, four men died at Ruby Trust Mine and another slide destroyed cabins at Richardson's Camp.[225]

Major threats came from the United States and the Chicago slides at the Camp Bird. These slides took lives in 1906, 1911, 1936, and 1958. The United States Slide in 1906 buried four and killed three when it hit the mill and then ran on to the boardinghouse. Further avalanche danger forced two hundred miners to take refuge in the mine's adit. The 1911 slide killed four men and their pack teams on the road to Camp Bird. In 1936, three died when a slide carried off several buildings, and in 1958 four more died on the road to the mine.[226]

Nestled between the San Juan Mountains to the east and the San Miguel Mountains to the west, Telluride is one of the most beautiful

Waterhole Slide at Camp Bird near Ouray around 1900. This team and driver were caught and buried. Another team had already been covered. Only in the spring melt were they recovered. (Ouray Historical Society)

mountain valleys anywhere. Telluride is remote and difficult to reach. Sometimes it had its rowdy moments, but it was usually peaceful. West of Telluride a giant tram carried ore three miles from the Liberty Bell Mine high in Cornet Basin. This large mine operation had backing from Eastern capitalists, and careful planning went into the mine's development, its workings, and the accommodations for miners. In 1899 Kansas City investors leased the mine with railroad promoter A. E. Stilwell as president of the Liberty Bell Gold Mining Company. Before these latest owners took control the Liberty Bell Mine had a lackluster career, but the new management made it one of the big producers of the Telluride district close behind the Smuggler-Union and the Tomboy. In 1901 the effective Resident Manager, J. W. Mercer, took leave and left for Ecuador to manage mines owned by the Vanderbilts, his expertise needed there for developing better methods of treating ore. In his absence Arthur Winslow, the general manager and consultant for the Kansas City Company came out to manage operations at the Liberty Bell Mine. The ore bodies developed under the new management were wide and uniformly high in gold and silver content. Impressive workings had been built to process the ore for shipment to Telluride. The mill had a large capacity and was connected to Telluride by a three-mile long Blichert tramway. The mill had stamps, Wilfley Tables and cyanide bleaching vats. Over 150 men worked in the mine and mill on the day of the avalanche.[227]

Managers took into account the possibility of an avalanche when choosing a site for the boardinghouse. The mine owners provided accommodations for a crew of up to 250 men since the three-mile trail from Telluride was steep, rugged, avalanche-prone, and sometimes impassable in winter. They carefully surveyed and studied the hills, benches and valleys in the vicinity of the Liberty Bell Mine. Planners even interviewed old-timers about the nature and places where avalanches had run over the years to assist in making a decision on a suitable and safe location. The site chosen was on a level piece of ground close to the mine tunnel that seemed safe since no slides had ever come that way. Old growth trees had stood undisturbed for hundreds of years on Greenback Mountain that towered over the mine, mill, and boardinghouse. Near the top of the mountain there were cliffs that usually deflected avalanches to gulches on each side of the bench where the boardinghouse sat. Still, planners knew avalanches could be unpredictable and added extra protection by constructing the building with expensive heavy timbers and anchoring the structure with thick wire rope secured by bolts driven into solid rock. For a few years the boardinghouse stood unmolested.

A bleak and snowy day dawned February 28, 1902, in the San Juan Mountains, as it had for nearly two weeks. The worst snowstorm in memory raged over the San Juans. More snow fell than even in the record storm of 1899, and it increased in intensity over three or four days. Accompanied by high winds, deep drifts formed in every gulch and depression. Small avalanches ran regularly.[228] Rio Grande Southern traffic all but stopped. The storm isolated Telluride, but the mines kept working at Pandora, the Smuggler-Union, Tomboy, and Liberty Bell although some people feared an impending doom.

Shortly after seven a.m. the night shift turned in at the Liberty Bell bunkhouse while the day shift miners filed into the dining room for breakfast. At the nearby stables, L. M. Ulmstead harnessed animals for a day's work hauling ore from the crusher to the tram station. Mr. Ulmstead was routinely cinching harnesses when he heard a crashing and terrifying sound. The avalanche hit without warning and turned three heavily constructed buildings into splinters. Down Cornet Gulch the avalanche continued carrying pieces of buildings 2,000 feet down the mountainside. With great anxiety Ulmstead peeked out the stable door, afraid to see what had happened. From the stable shadows he saw a tram cable swinging with the ore buckets flung off and rolling down the hillside. He looked toward the boardinghouse and saw only splintered timber ends sticking up from the ground. Mr. Ulmstead made his way to the where the tram house had stood and noticed coveralls poking up through the debris. He tugged at the denim trousers and pulled out the first victim found of the Liberty Bell slide — Gus Kraul's lifeless body.

The Liberty Bell avalanche started nearly one-half mile up the mountainside and descended so quickly that no one had time to move out of its way. It passed over the protective cliffs without hesitation and uprooted tree trunks three feet in diameter. Smaller trees were ground into splinters. Huge boulders yanked from the ground floated along on a snow mass seventy-five feet wide. One survivor reported that the sky " . . . grew dark and the air was filled with a noise as if a hundred cannons were bursting." The avalanche lifted and flung the horrified man through the air a hundred feet down the slope. A snowbank broke his fall and he ended his terrible ride uninjured. The air cleared and after recovering his senses he saw below " . . . the wreckage, snow, and bodies piled high in Cornet gulch."[229]

Three large buildings lay strewn in the valley. Bodies lay among and underneath debris and prevented an accurate count of victims. A first estimate placed the death toll at forty. The gully quickly earned the epithet "death gulch." In its destructive course the avalanche knocked down telephone lines, severing all communication to Telluride. Many people had seen or heard it from a distance and sounded the alarm. As the news was conveyed by word-of-mouth a continuous line of men armed with pick, shovel, and dynamite wound their way up the rugged trail to the disaster.[230] Survivors set to work recovering those buried. Quick action saved a dozen miners' lives. As hope began to return that more men could be saved a second slide came down and caught twenty-four rescuers. Survivors frantically searched for even more Liberty Bell victims. Then, horror upon horror, a third avalanche fell on searchers. If the devil lives, then he lived at the Liberty Bell that day. Just an hour later a fourth slide buried several searchers. Those who escaped alive returned to the grim search. Their heroic efforts saved most of the buried rescuers and several more of the earlier victims. Some had serious injuries including one man with a severed arm. At long last the mine superintendent called off the search to avoid further casualties. Seven died in the final three slides.[231] Before an accurate estimate of the number missing from the boardinghouse could be determined, the rescuers themselves suffered a very high price. An unknown number of men remained hidden beneath the terrible white mass.

Searchers in several groups started down the steep winding trail to Telluride. At Curve Station, a direction change for the tram, a slide had snared and killed four men. Later a fifth body surfaced near the same spot.[232] By day's end an estimated twenty to thirty victims had died or disappeared.

The next day armed guards closed the trail to everyone until authorities could complete precautionary measures. Heavy posts were driven high above the disaster site to deflect slides away from the search area and give rescuers some confidence. They set off dynamite charges in the snowpack on the mountain to bring down or stabilize any remaining weaknesses. Only then did searchers resume the body recovery work.

Volunteers kept paying the highest price for their efforts. A report told of John Johns, a miner at Sheridan Mine of the Smuggler-Union complex, who stepped out of the boardinghouse on his way to help Liberty Bell victims when an avalanche swept him to his death. More news of the missing and killed arrived with warnings of greater impending danger.[233] One searcher looked above at the heavy snow overhangs and made the comment " . . . It will be down on us next . . ."[234] Then " . . . a slight rumbling which broke into a thundering roar, a sound which will make the strongest quail, the huge mountain of snow came down the cliff dealing death in its track."[235] Little more could be done. Too many had died. Word went out to Telluride "send no more help." If possible, searchers brought bodies to town or wrapped and placed them in a safe location until transport could be arranged. Before heading into town the Liberty Bell searchers uncovered Gus Von Fintel's and Paul Zelbra's bodies just inches below the surface. By then two prominent citizens had lost their lives in rescue work at Liberty Bell Mine. Gus Rohwer and William Gregory died along with their horses the moment they arrived on the first day. Within a twenty-four hour period these disasters produced a score of widows and dozens of orphans.[236]

On the third day several more slides flew down the gulches around Telluride. Avalanches stripped the Bobtail Mine buildings into the valley below. Soon after the feared Pandora avalanche, among the area's largest avalanches, slid destructively. Witnesses noted that the:

> . . . *first slide occurred this morning and destroyed the mill of the Smuggler-Union Mining company at Pandora and the residences of the foreman, Z. W. Van Low. Messrs. Van Low, A. P. Blarney and O. M. Sackett had homes near the mill, but owing to the dangerous conditions these men had removed their families to places of safety.*
>
> *[Soon after] . . . the first slide at Pandora about forty people from Telluride went to the scene of the disaster, and while they were working there a second slide came and killed at least three people, although there may have been others caught . . . This second slide also destroyed the tension station of the Smuggler-Union mine.*[237]

Mine managers called off this search as well as the one at Liberty Bell mine.

The high mountains surrounding Telluride on three sides continued to threaten inhabitants. Never had so much snow covered the ground or had cornices grown so large at the crest of windswept ridges. A trigger such as a cornice falling or a sudden wind rush could bring wholesale destruction upon Telluride. Owners closed their mines. Miners and families retreated to town for refuge or perhaps to die together.

This storm pounded all San Juan Mountain areas. Across the San Miguel range to the west of Telluride, the Gold King Mine closed. Miners rode ore buckets down to safety in Ophir. No sooner had they arrived than a tremendous avalanche took out a large section of the tram. Rumors spread that an avalanche had buried twenty people just east of Telluride on Red Mountain's Sunnyside Mine. Reports of avalanches killing people as they fled to reach the safety of a town came from Silverton and Ouray. The railroads ground to a stop.

Near Telluride the storm cut off six or seven men in Ingram Basin from all communication. Ingram Basin experienced frequent avalanches even in normal years, caused by leeward snow loading and the hazardous repose of gulches. A search party formed to look for the isolated group. Searchers climbed a steep precipice toward the mine while people in town watched expecting the snow-covered hillside to cut loose and kill the searchers. After this party had left officials posted armed guards at trail and road heads to stop others from going into the hazardous back country.

Smuggler-Union Mine in 1902 after being covered by an avalanche. Hours before, the superintendent of the mine ordered the miners to evacuate to Telluride in response to the tragedy of the Liberty Bell disaster that killed nineteen. (Denver Public Library, Western History Department)

Many remained missing at Liberty Bell. Some men volunteered to build a temporary boardinghouse. Authorities allowed them to make their way to the scene, but armed guards stopped others. Before construction could begin they needed to control two large intimidating slide paths. They positioned a lookout to give a warning shot in case of sudden movement. Workmen laid dynamite in strategic places and set it off creating avalanches that hopefully would be the last. This preventative measure stabilized the remaining snowpack.[238] After eight days a new boardinghouse stood and sheltered a hundred searchers.

Nearby in Bear Creek Basin Jack Nixon and Reddin Bougher received a visit from the "White Death." A tremendous slide ripped their cabin from the ground and sent it down the mountainside. While avalanches crashed by them on every side rescuers struggled to reach the two men. Twelve rescuers found Nixon's and Bougher's remains.

Trenching, probing, and plain digging proceeded for several days at Liberty Bell Mine until hope of finding any victims alive disappeared. The final count came to nineteen dead at the Liberty Bell Mine and many more throughout the region.

A period of grief and mourning followed in Telluride. Soon after rescue efforts ended, accusations began to fly and the search for someone to blame got underway. General Manager Arthur Winslow grieved over so many lost and tried to explain how owners and supervisors took great care selecting the building site for the Liberty Bell boardinghouse:

> . . . *Never before, or in twenty years at least, . . . has a snowslide reached the place where our buildings stood. I inquired into this matter of the course of slides when selecting a site for the buildings at our upper workings, and it was after a careful canvass of the subject that we decided on the location, which is a flat about 200 by 400 feet and in the timber —* . . . *We took every precaution possible to safeguard our employees as well as our expensive improvements, and the disaster is a work of nature with which human ingenuity was unable to cope.*[239]

Manager Winslow created a fund to provide emergency care for many of the widows and orphans. The Telluride City Council provided funding for rescue work and victims' funeral expenses. Mourning for so many lost lasted a long time in this tightly-knit community. Mine Inspector P. H. Clifford attempted to make some sense of it all when he commented that:

. . . the disastrous snowslide . . . throws to the winds all theories and disregards entirely the precedent evolved out of ancient experience with reference to the most feared of all dangers in mountain life, snowslides.

Now it is shown that these slides are liable to occur from any direction. The ill-fated bunkhouse was situated snugly in Cornet basin, into which Cornet gulch running up the mountain from Telluride, opens. This basin is about two and a half or three miles from the town; not as the crow flies, but as the trail, which is tortuous as all mountain trails are, goes. This basin widens to from 600 to 1,000 and 2,000 feet, with high projecting mountains all around it.

The bunkhouse was on a kind of bench or flat piece of country, some distance from the steep grade of the mountain.

The bunkhouse was supposed to be in a safe place, because it was not in line with either track of the snowslides of the past. It was placed on the ridge for the very reason that all conceded it to be the securest point on the mountain. Never in the memory of the oldest inhabitant did a snowslide come that way. It was plain, too, from the fact that trees stood directly ahead that no slide had ever traversed the course during the life of the trees.

. . . To the trained eye of the mountaineer it is not difficult to find the danger line. In the path of snowslides these are the marks of destruction and barren desolation conspicuous even on a rock-ribbed mountainside. These points are shunned as the breath of pestilence or the lair of wild beasts. There are dangers enough in wild mountain life, but the snowslide comprises all of the elements of terror combined. It comes without warning and there is no escape even for the wary. . . . But it could be seen that none ever came down this part of the mountain in which the bunkhouse of the Liberty Bell lay. There were the two regular paths of the slides on either side, plain enough, but they were at a safe distance from the humble home of the sub-terra toilers.[240]

This extended catastrophe caused twenty-six avalanche fatalities in and around Telluride. It added a terrible footnote to events of the past year that left many families mourning and created a political rift in the community. The previous summer, a fire at Smuggler-Union Mine had killed twenty-four. About that same time a strike created ill feelings between miners and owners.[241] Governor Orman had called Colorado's National Guard to quell disturbances. Adding insult and anguish to the suffering survivors, Colorado State National Guard

Commander, Adjutant General George F. Gardner, called the Telluride disasters a signal from "The Maker" to miners for their sins against mine owners. Labor leaders asked Governor Orman to remove Gardner from office. Gardner denied the statements and Orman absolved him of any guilt.[242]

The terror at Telluride ended and the families buried their dead. Those who lost a wage earner suffered the most. Some stayed on and reestablished their lives. Others left to establish new lives or returned to their families, usually in the East. The Liberty Bell victims were: Gus Swanson, F. C. Clemmer, Gus Von Fintel, George Rohwer, W. S. Gregory, H. S. Summerland, Harry Golden, Gus Kraul, Raymond Bishop, Wade Crowe, Harry A. Chase, L. D. Stanley, J. R. Powell, Paul Dalpra, Olof Swanson, J. G. Cedarberg, Louie Lundberg, Andrew Aho, and an unknown boy.

Telluride has not experienced such a disaster since that winter of 1902. But just three years later another winter with unusually heavy snows brought the San Juan mining region another round of avalanche disasters.

CHAPTER 6

❅

Winter of 1905–1906

> *A score of lives have been lost and property valued at hundreds of thousands of dollars destroyed in snowslides which have swept the mountains within the last few days. In the San Juan district the loss has been the greatest.* — Rocky Mountain News, *March 20, 1906.*[243]

The severe winter of 1905-1906 resembled the "Big Snow" year of 1899. Heavy snow and numerous avalanches caused many deaths and large-scale property damage. Inclement weather created one of the highest fatality periods in a single year. Weather conditions produced avalanche conditions everywhere in Colorado, but in the avalanche triangle of Ouray, Silverton, and Telluride the highest statistics mounted.[244] In the San Juan region the steep valleys and confined gulches topped by large catchment basins near the peak summits posed the greatest danger. Added to these factors was a series of storms that produced heavy snowfall that piled deep onto an already unstable base. In a single storm late in 1905 twelve feet of snow fell.[245] Such heavy snowfall caused serious avalanche danger all over the San Juans.

Everywhere in Colorado the heavy snow and drifting interrupted communication and endangered mines, camps, railroads, and towns. On Mount Bross, a 14,000-foot peak near Fairplay in South Park, John Dunne and his partner, George W. Shelton, picked and shoveled their way along while attempting to open the trail to their mine — the Privateer. John Dunne became the first fatality recorded that season. The men's work set off the slide that carried Dunne 2,000 feet down the mountain. Shelton grabbed a large rock outcropping and managed to hold on as the snow slid away around him. After the slide passed he searched for his partner but was unable to save him.[246]

Harry Youmans, Otto Bowers, and Fred Davidson were breaking a path through the snow in Nellie Gulch near Lake City. The men stood on a plank pulled by mules to pack the snow so that wagons of lumber could be hauled from their sawmill. With Youmans driving and the other men behind them, they came to the threatening avalanche path that sometimes ran after storms. They paused for a moment to assess the danger but decided since they were in the bottom of the gulch that their movement along its base was safe. The moment they started the slide was undercut and descended. Seeing the slide break high above, the men jumped off and ran to the creek bottom and up the opposite side. Bowers made it farthest up the mountain and was only partially buried. He also had the good fortune of still having his shovel and managed to free himself and Youmans. Immediately they set about looking for Davidson. William Stapley had come along soon after the slide and made a quick trip to Henson and Lake City to sound the alarm. Youmans and Bowers could hear Davidson's call for help but could not pinpoint the location from where it came. Working to exhaustion the men dug to find their companion but the sounds became fainter and finally stopped. Still they frantically searched hoping to find Davidson with some breath of life left in him. After an hour and a half of excavating they found Davidson, but too late, as his body had already cooled and no breath frosted the air. Every effort was made to revive him but to no avail. By the time a large force of men arrived from camps in every direction Davidson had been found. The two mules were also found dead.

In the Crystal River mining district the narrow gauge grades were built along streams and in basins and therefore passed below several avalanche paths. These trains provided the main transportation link between towns and the mines up Roaring Fork tributaries in Elk Mountain Range that included the Crystal River. Several avalanches struck at life and property in the winter of 1906.

In mid-January, fatal avalanches transpired at Coal Basin near Aspen. Three miners left the workings about noon and followed a trail to their homes. Their families anxiously awaited them knowing that avalanches had been running in the area during the last twenty-four hours. When none of the miners arrived by evening an alarm was sounded and searchers trekked out to find the men. As they made their way toward the mine they came to a spot where an avalanche had completely obscured the trail. Footprints could be seen entering at the uphill edge, but none exited from the other side. Searchers trenched and dug until late that night until they found all three bodies.[247]

Around March 13, 1906, Coal Basin residents heard and saw avalanches in the surrounding area. With great fear they remembered the men who were lost two months earlier and residents decided to evacuate the area. Once on board a Denver and Rio Grande train they felt relieved and secure. Pulling away from the station the coaches gently rocked as the train traveled across majestic mountainsides lulling the passengers into a deep sleep. Then without warning an avalanche struck the train on the way to Carbondale and buried a coach occupied by eighteen miners, a woman, and a child. The coach overturned, but no one received serious injury. Avalanches continued to run all around the stalled train at a rate of about one per hour completely burying it and the derailed engine. Filled with fear, the passengers dug out and walked to Redstone and safety. The next day all boarded another train, and with the tracks cleared overnight traveled to Carbondale.

Meanwhile back in Coal Basin a clerk escaped injury when a slide hit the Colorado Supply store where he worked. The same slide hit a pipeline and then continued on to the railroad grade and knocked five loaded cars off the track.[248]

At Silverton a slide barreled down and hit the Old Hundred Mine property on Galena Mountain. Four miles from Eureka five Italian miners lost their lives at Sunnyside Mine on January 22.[249] An avalanche had caught them when they were endeavoring to cut a path through snow to the tunnel entrance.[250] Slides at Rico blocked several engines between there and Ames. Near Telluride, slides blocked the Rio Grande Southern rails and between Durango and Silverton avalanches closed the route on the Denver and Rio Grande.[251] At Silverton one slide dammed the Animas River backing water up for hundreds of feet. Trains were frozen to the track for more than a week before they could again move over this section.[252] South of Silverton slides and drifts on the Denver and Rio Grande closed the railroad in many places leaving no outlet to Durango. Manual labor and rotary plows cleared most of the blockage and the Rio Grande Railroad returned to service within hours of its first closures.[253] At Animas Forks a Kendall Mountain avalanche buried miners Peter Magunson and Charles Gustafson near the Bagley Tunnel. It reached Silverton's town limits, and destroyed several houses along its course.[254]

Heavy snow fell during the third week of January. Mines closed operations and traffic halted along roads and railroads. Slides raged continually in the "avalanche triangle." One slide knocked a stagecoach, driver, passengers, and the four-horse team off the road near Ironton. Riders, driver, and horses survived.[255]

Colorado's snowiest month of the year is March, and this proved true when about mid-month a strong storm made an appearance. Mines, roads, and railroads were closed isolating many towns in the southwest and elsewhere in the state. Reports read like a repeat of 1899 with the Alpine Tunnel blocked by slides, Crested Butte and surrounding communities blocked by drifts and slides, and the Rio Grande Southern barricaded by snow. The railroad to Crystal River and Coal Basin was covered by avalanches and was closed. Trains through South Park moved with great difficulty.[256]

Just west of the Alpine Tunnel a train became snowbound. Crews had to stay and keep boiler pressure up since it took many hours, and sometimes days, to bring huge boilers to steam. For sixteen days the men braved the elements. The railroad sent a rotary and crew from Como to clear a path on each side of Alpine Tunnel yet the rotary soon was hopelessly stuck. Management then dispatched fifty men to dig out the rotary, but soon after arriving the group heard an avalanche start high above. Dropping their shovels they rushed to find safety. It missed most of them, but a few were slightly injured by flying debris. The slide settled in at 300 feet wide and fifty feet deep. Along its path it had snapped huge trees and carried along giant boulders. The effort to free the rotary had to wait until better conditions returned.[257]

On the western side a train tried coming up the grade from Pitkin to the Alpine Tunnel. Within a mile of the stranded crew the relief train stuck fast in a drift. The crews began a long and laborious effort of hauling food and coal on foot to sustain the appetites of men and machine. Finally after sixteen days a rotary from Gunnison cut through drifts and freed the crew and train.[258]

At the same time in the Sawatch Range in Clear Creek district at Winfield:

> *. . . a serious condition exists. North and west the moun-*
> *tains tower above the little camp nearly perpendicular. Snow*
> *many feet deep covers them and at their crest a comb of*
> *snow and ice hangs ready to start on its death dealing mis-*
> *sion at any moment. The lack of telephone or telegraph lines*
> *makes it impossible to reach them for news and much appre-*
> *hension is felt for their safety.*[259]

Apprehension became reality when four miles east of Winfield a huge avalanche started above Vicksburg. Residents stated it was 3,000 feet wide and ran a course of over four miles in length clearing the old growth timber from the mountainside. Winfield folks never knew of any such slide ever happening at Vicksburg. In its course a gully three hundred feet deep had no effect on the mass as it jumped the depression with ease. It continued to the valley floor carrying off Harry Wiesenborn's cabin along with a piece of a huge flume. It filled the valley floor to a depth of nearly 300 feet. Searchers from the frightened town of Winfield where deadly slides had visited in the past skied to Vicksburg to look for survivors. They feared the slide had caught Wiesenborn and maybe others. When they arrived at Vicksburg res- cuers encountered massive debris, and their hearts sank with the real- ization that little hope existed of finding anyone alive in such a huge expanse. A relatively short search revealed Harry Wiesenborn's body, but not the others. They returned to Winfield surrounded by its snow- covered and corniced peaks, and the fear of an even worse avalanche concerned all. With the road east out of the valley blocked at Vicksburg, Winfield residents waited out the danger. Time passed and no further tragedy visited upon Clear Creek district that year.[260] Spring came and the search for bodies resumed.[261]

In the next drainage north of Winfield in Black Cloud Canyon a slide seriously injured Frank Ryan but spared his partner at a mine above Twin Lakes. Ryan's partner ran into the tunnel just as the ava- lanche came down. Several miners heard it and hurried to give aid. They found Ryan quickly because he yelled for help, but by the time rescuers cleared away the snow Ryan had slipped into unconsciousness. Then they dug the partner out of his safe place inside the tunnel. He suffered mostly from fright. Ryan later died of his injuries.[262]

In the southwest an avalanche scared Liberty Bell miners west of Telluride. A slide rushed down the same path as the deadly 1902 avalanche that killed nineteen. This time it caught no one but destroyed the upper tram terminal and several towers. A supervisor wasted no time evacuating the camp.

Nearby various slides destroyed the blacksmith shop and other buildings of the Smuggler-Union Mine's Bullion Tunnel. On Red Mountain, a slide destroyed buildings at the Joker Tunnel. At the Morning Star Mine in Milk Creek a slide partially crushed the boardinghouse, but timbers held up well enough for people to safely dig out.[263] Near Ophir slides hemmed in a train crew and knocked down telephone lines leaving loved ones in fear for their safety.[264] Up valley from Camp Bird people only guessed the fate of Revenue's 200 miners located in line with the threatening Potosi slide. They took refuge in the mine tunnel. With communications cut off everyone dreaded the worst for all of the Sneffels district miners.[265] In other San Juan areas, slides produced damage, injury, and several fatalities. At Animas Forks, near Silverton, and at Telluride power lines chopped by slides imperiled miners and families. One report said a slide engulfed a train at Ophir Loop killing thirty-five, but the Rio Grande Southern replied with a report that there was no train in the vicinity at the time of the slide. The storm eventually let up on the Sneffels district allowing rescue parties to relieve those stranded at the Revenue Mine Tunnel and other properties.

In Cunningham Gulch near Silverton on March 17 two separate avalanches destroyed the Green Mountain Mill and Unity Tunnel boardinghouse at the foot of St. John's Mountain. These incidents killed three.[266]

Adolph Hellene failed to arrive in Silverton as expected. His friends discussed if they should go out and look for him with avalanche danger being so extreme. After a wait and hoping that conditions had improved a group started skiing to Hellene's cabin. The searchers found the worst possible situation. A huge avalanche covered an area so large and deep that his friends could not even locate the cabin. They returned to Silverton saddened by the loss of a dear friend. A few days later he showed up in town and related his story.

During the onslaught of snowfall he said he had no trouble sleeping believing that his stout cabin would protect him from a devastating slide. Suddenly he awoke startled at what sounded like a freight train running by the house. Quick to his feet he tried to look outside, but snow blocked the door. Windows were white with snow packed tightly against panes. Snow covered the chimney and smoke began filling the room. Hellene managed to force his door open enough to start digging. All night and on into afternoon he dug until he finally broke out. The slide covered the cabin to a depth of forty feet. During this ordeal his friends had reached the site. After probing and trenching for a time they left without even locating the cabin or realizing that he toiled below. Ascending from his tomb Hellene regained his senses to the world around. He heard avalanches cracking and booming on peaks in every direction. His senses indicated that travel could be dangerous. With plenty of provisions he waited in safety for a few days until the snow settled.[267]

While friends of Hellene's toasted his safe return to them in Silverton a report came of an avalanche down in Cunningham Gulch.[268] The working people of the avalanche triangle soon faced a more gruesome catastrophe.

George Howard had built a cabin at the mouth of Cunningham Gulch that became the core of Howardsville five miles north of Silverton.[269] Howard established the town ten years after Baker first prospected the area now called Baker's Park. The Little Giant Mine in Arrastra Gulch was the first important ore body in the area. A water-powered arrastra ground ore into powder, and then miners used pan or sluice boxes to separate the gold.[270] Howardsville became San Juan County's first county seat. It had the first brewery, post office, assay office, saloon, and blacksmith shop in the area.[271] Shortly after establishment of San Juan County, Silverton citizens enticed Howardsville officials to join them for a celebration. When the Howardsville group was sufficiently drunk, Silverton folks stole the county records and moved them to Silverton. A vote was quickly held and Silverton was voted in as the new county seat.[272] The pioneers of this district were not immune to the "White Death" and no day proved it more than March 19, 1906.

On the east slope of King Solomon Mountain above Cunningham Gulch at the *daughter of the stars* — Shenandoah Mine — two dozen miners sat for dinner. Ten more men slept overhead on the second-story floor. After a week of snow the skies cleared and temperatures began to rise. With no warning an avalanche started high above in a glacial cirque. It came down silently and struck carrying away a large portion of the boardinghouse. It crushed the tramway and collateral buildings like eggshells. It dropped into Cunningham Gulch running to the valley floor and struck the Green Mountain Mill killing Foreman Daniel R. Hickey. At the Shenandoah Mine twelve men, some with injuries, dug themselves out. The ten sleeping in the loft received no injuries. Twelve more lay buried. Manager Hill escaped but wandered disoriented throughout the night until found fevered from exposure and with badly-frozen feet.

Rescue efforts could not begin because travel anywhere from Silverton would probably have meant death. Just before this event sev-

The Shenandoah avalanche of 1906 claimed twelve lives at the mine. Three of the victims have been brought from the mine thousands of feet above the Green Mountain Mill seen here damaged by the same avalanche. A mill operator inside was killed bringing the total to thirteen fatalities. (San Juan Historical Society)

eral mines had been closed and 3,000 miners risked the journey from remote locations and crowded into Silverton. Starvation faced the district as trains, blocked by avalanches of Rio Grande tracks from Durango, had to stay in their yard unable to bring in supplies. The Iowa slide at the edge of Silverton crashed down and barricaded railroad tracks increasing the possibility of starvation. Despite the danger of leaving Silverton, the organization of a rescue became first priority. Throwing caution aside a large party made its way up Cunningham Gulch and the steep trail to Shenandoah.

When rescuers arrived theirs hearts sank at the sight of the flattened boardinghouse and news of the twelve buried miners. For hours they dug, trenched, and probed finding seven bodies. As days went by the searching continued. March came to a close and a warm period began melting some of the slide. Hundreds of feet down the canyon the remaining bodies surfaced.[273]

The dead were: Jacob Theboldt, Jesse Shaw, Gus Heise, Peter Coleburg, Bert Albert, Edward Kirk, Slate Branton, Emil Bos, three whose first names were unknown — Gustavson, Margelo, Piccolo — and one unknown man.[274]

One of the survivors of the Shenandoah avalanche, W. N. "Bill" Hall, wrote a poem to the survivors, and in honor of the dead:

Shenandoah Slide

Down the canyon where the Shenandoah cast her gloom
There they settled
Twenty-one miners who were happy as could be
Never had a cross word, and on all questions did agree.

We were sitting warm and cozy,
And were thinking of the time
When we'd meet our wives and sweethearts
In the Good Old Summer Time.

But, we were caught in a snowslide,
While we reckoned on our might,
And were carried down the canyon
On that fatal St. Patrick's night.

Nine of us escaped, most, perished,
But the others we did not know
Whether they'd see another sun rise
Or were buried in the snow.

We wandered around for hours
Where we were going, we did not know,
But by good fortune we were landed in the tunnel
And were safe from all the snow.

When daylight came we searched for our companions -
Where they were we did not know,
But the truth soon became apparent
They had perished in the snow.

But we hope sometime to meet them,
Where there'll be no more of woe
And the place will always be sunshine
And there will be no more snow.[275]

Avalanches elsewhere tore buildings from foundations and carried debris down steep mountainsides sometimes to valley floors. Starvation loomed in many areas, as relief parties could not dig through drifts and avalanches. Snowdrifts and slides continued to temporarily block trains.[276] At Creede an avalanche ran down Mammoth Mountain in the late afternoon of March 19, demolishing the East Willow Mining Company Mill and killing Samuel East. It carried large timbers across the gulch two hundred feet, driving some timbers into hard rock cliffs.[277] At the Sunlight Mine near Animas Forks a slide killed two.[278] At Eureka's Silver Wing Mine, slides killed one man and badly injured another. Slides overcame the Mountain Queen Mine engine room burying two but both survived. Avalanches completely destroyed the Highland Mary buildings, but Providence smiled and numerous miners and personnel walked away uninjured.

Relief finally came on March 22 when the storms ended and the settling of the snowpack began. Searchers throughout the San Juans fanned out looking for those believed lost or caught in slides. At Bonner Mine properties the body of one of two men killed was found. Others were found safe at mines, or on trails, as they attempted to come into towns.

Rio Grande crews toiled at Elk Park south of Silverton clearing an avalanche 3800 feet long. Opening the road over Red Mountain Pass was slow. The Riverside slide, seven miles south of Ouray, ran in two places. Crews cut a tunnel and trench to open this stage and freight wagon route.[279] In Sneffels district the Camp Bird Mine received a visit.

The Sneffels district west of Ouray is one of the most avalanche-prone regions in the country. Some of the most productive mines in the country were in the district including the Revenue, Virginius, Banker's National, and Camp Bird. These mines produced millions of dollars in silver and gold. Over the years avalanches destroyed property and took lives. Many stories exist describing the effect heavy snow and avalanches had on those who mined, drove teams, or in one case, carried the United States mail. A mail carrier, Gene Bell, related his story of being caught on the route to Camp Bird in 1892:

> *. . . when along comes one of those pesky blankets which are not only wet and cold but durned dangerous as well to man and beast. It just lifted my horse and me out of our accustomed way of going and when we had time to look about I was in a creek bed at the foot of a gulch and the horse — well, God knows where it was.*
>
> *Not far away was a tunnel, out of which was pouring a steady stream of water. I know things were melting, and my only hope was that water would wash away the unexpected house I had been furnished with. For twenty-four hours I stood up without being able to turn, just hedged in as if in my coffin.*[280]

Camp Bird boardinghouse after the 1906 avalanche. Notice the tunnel made through the building. Miners asleep on the upper floor were rudely awakened but none were injured. (Denver Public Library, Western History Department)

Breezeway made by the 1906 Camp Bird avalanche. (Denver Public Library, Western History Department)

Eventually the water rushing from the tunnel melted away ice and snow from around Gene and he was free to continue his rounds.

The United States Avalanche in Mount Sneffels district six miles south of Ouray threatened the Camp Bird often. On March 18, 1906, at 1:00 a.m., after extreme snowfall loaded old snowpack, the United States avalanche ran. Usually it stopped short of the mine workings, but this time it descended all the way to the mine hitting the mill, and a portion of the tramway.[281] Although recently built at a cost of $400,000, the mill's being hit may have been a blessing. Owing to the mill's massive size, it slowed and absorbed the slide's energy and may have lessened damage and loss of life.[282] In a further twist of fate the mill's destruction was completed when it burned down March 20. This completely threw mine employees out of work until the London-based owners of the property could decide if they would rebuild the mill.

One boardinghouse had a hole poked completely through its walls and was moved off its foundation. In another boardinghouse the avalanche buried four but all survived. These men might have died without the avalanche-resistant architecture. The house was later moved back onto its foundation and cabled to solid rock to keep it from moving again.

Three men in the mill were not so lucky. The slide hit the mill full force trapping them inside.[283] A Ouray County commissioner saw the destruction while on route to the mine late that night. It took him all night to struggle back to Ouray, raise the alarm, and organize a rescue party. Rescuers started toward Camp Bird, but the storm conditions increased causing them to turn back until the weather subsided. Finally rescuers broke a path and made it to the tragic site to begin searching. The four buried in the boardinghouse were found alive, but after hours of digging the three people in the mill were discovered dead.

Destruction of the Camp Bird Mill in the 1906 avalanche probably kept fatalities low. The slide hit the mill first dissipating much of its power before striking the populated areas with boardinghouses and houses. A few days later the mill burned to the ground. (Ouray Historical Society)

All over the San Juans, reports came in that avalanches descended on mines, camps, towns, and trains. Many slides blocked roads and cut telephone service. The Revenue Mine in the valley below Mount Sneffels was no exception. In the Sneffels district, which included Camp Bird, the Revenue, and Banker's National Mine, as many as 600 miners found themselves stranded and facing death by starvation.[284] More hardship came after an avalanche took out a transformer of the

Animas and Telluride Power Company that brought electrical service over the range from Telluride.[285]

The plight of the 250 miners stranded at Camp Bird worried Ouray townsfolk. Before another rescue party could reach the camp a second slide fell at six that evening and destroyed the stamp mill, two storehouses, tram house, ten tram towers, and two miles of tram cable. The men took refuge in the mine tunnel just after the first slide, but faced starvation because the second slide destroyed the warehouse. Several men from the famed Ashenfelter Transportation Company worked to open the road to the Camp Bird. They reached the camp but only evacuated three injured men before deciding further rescue efforts too risky.[286] People at the scene estimated snow-drifts piled sixty feet around Camp Bird, and higher in the Imogene Basin — some up to 300 feet deep.[287]

Eventually the storm ended and a final series of slides brought danger to an end as snowpack settled and stabilized. People found the missing miners, cleared the mine and mill wreckage, and reopened the roads and railroads. It was a year of high fatalities and perhaps the worst for property damage. Slides killed at least eighteen in San Juan County alone. They counted mills, aerial trams, and boardinghouses among the expensive workings brought down by avalanches.[288] Nature has never repeated a year such as the winter of 1905-1906.

A year later on March 17, 1907, at Camp Bird, a slide annihilated several houses, buildings, and the mill. This happened before and would happen again. Nearby on the road to Camp Bird, another slide carried off a half-dozen six-horse wagon teams, the drivers and a stagecoach. The force of the air blast knocked down a horse and rider a half mile away. A gold-filled strongbox on the stagecoach blew off and has never been recovered.[289]

The twentieth century brought the world new technological wonders including the automobile that made possible mobility for the common man as never known before. Mining declined and the Colorado Mountains emptied of much of their population. Avalanches continued to take a toll on life but gradually the numbers of people most exposed changed from those who worked in the mountains to those who visited for recreation activities using the freedom the automobile gave. Deaths have been fewer in numbers but the tragedy continues, made both more dangerous — but ironically more safe — by technology.

CHAPTER 7

After the Frontier:
Avalanches in the Twentieth Century

Dry slides occur when hard, granular snow falls. Each round pellet of snow acts like a roller bearing. A wind starts them rolling and they pick up others in their path until tons of snow, carrying rocks and trees with it, is given a momentum that nothing can stop.[290] — Article in Denver Post, *February 18, 1936, describing how snow conditions may have developed to cause the Hesperus Mine disaster.*

The western frontier was considered closed in 1890 when the last homestead was claimed and the open range was enclosed with barbed wire. With the start of World War I mining revived as old mines reopened and producing mines expanded to provide the strategic minerals needed for the war effort. After World War I some mines continued operating, but the days of boom and bust mining had come to an end. But Colorado would still boom in other economic areas. In the new century, recreation would see the old pattern of boom and bust as ski areas and towns grew overnight with some lasting a few years and others continuing to flourish to present times. The labor force after World War I was nonetheless just as vulnerable to avalanche catastrophe.

The Silver Jack Mine on the north slopes of Uncompahgre Peak showed great promise in the early twentieth century. The discoverer of the rich vein on the Cimarron River's east fork received financial backing and began building a trail to move in equipment. He planned to dam the Cimarron River upstream just below Uncompahgre Peak. A flume would be built to connect the dam with a concrete powerhouse at the Silver Jack Mine. Workers packed in supplies for this ambitious project by mule and construction work went on almost to completion. They finished the dam, flume, and two-story powerhouse, complete with turbines. Unfortunately, in this instance the San Juan Mountains proved that the works of man were no match for the ferocity of avalanches. In the spring, an avalanche came down, missed the powerhouse, and rode high up the opposite hillside. It hesitated a moment, reversed its course, only to return and flatten the powerhouse to the ground. Much of the mine machinery lay in ruins around the powerhouse and mine opening, some of it still crated waiting to be installed. The avalanche destroyed the investors' hopes and development never took place.[291]

A force of miners worked the Augusta Mine during the winter of 1904. It was February. Nine miners decided to take a break and pick up needed supplies in Crested Butte. Overnight clouds had deposited two feet of new snow on old snowpack. The superintendent urged his employees to wait a short time until others tossed dynamite sticks into the snow to check snowpack stability. Impatiently they ignored his urging and left. Six died in a massive slide.[292]

A second Woodstock avalanche occurred on February 8, 1909, a few months before a gas explosion in the Alpine Tunnel killed several men resulting in its closure forever. A train left Como with a rotary plow to clear the line through to Gunnison. After passing through the Alpine Tunnel the train ran into the upper debris of the avalanche downgrade from the Palisades along the same path of the 1884 slide path that killed thirteen. The rotary managed to pass through and clear the track continuing on around Sherrod Loop to the Woodstock spur. There the avalanche had settled 500 feet long and 40 feet deep at the center. Coming up the grade from Pitkin was a freight train loaded with food. The rotary attacked the slide through the first day and second but, when close to the middle, the snow was packed hard as ice rendering the rotary useless. The crews from both trains used picks and shovels to break pieces of the avalanche off the top and pushed them onto the track where the rotary could throw the debris off the grade. For seven days the crews worked the slide, shoveling snow into the boilers for water and chopping wood to the feed the fires. Finally the trains were able to pass each other and continued on their way.[293]

Few people actually died because of avalanches over the decades on the avalanche-prone route of the Rio Grande Southern. The exception was in 1912, when an avalanche caught a work crew trenching through a slide near Ophir. Another slide descended and buried twelve men. Survivors quickly started digging and soon found all of the men. Eight survived this deadly accident, but four died.[294]

The year 1916 was another big snow year. On Kelso Mountain in the Argentine district near Georgetown, U. S. Deputy Mineral Surveyor Arthur H. Osborne surveyed mining claims for Edward Collins and Ray Buckley who were assisting. Suddenly the snow broke away about thirty feet from above taking along Osborne and Collins. Buckley managed to scramble out of the slide's path. The avalanche carried the men down the steep mountain and into a narrow gulch for half a mile. Buckley searched for a while but could find no sign of the men. In despair he went to town and returned with forty men that night. For two days searching continued until the bodies of the men were finally uncovered.[295]

Near Chattanooga in the San Juan Mountains four years later sheepherders found a body near the Telescope Mine. Ten years before an avalanche disaster had visited the mine killing several people. All were found except the miner discovered in 1920. Apparently the man had been buried under debris and remained unseen until another slide came down and stripped away the debris that hid him.[296]

During the winter of 1916 heavier than usual snow blanketed the area around Twin Lakes. On January 23, nine avalanches ran on Mount Elbert in gulches above Twin Lakes. One of these hit the Gordon-Tiger Mine, on the same property where a slide killed a man and destroyed two buildings in 1899. In 1916 another avalanche struck while most of the miners:

> . . . *were engaged at work inside the tunnel, the ava-lanche ripped down the mountainside, tearing thru [sic] the blacksmith shop where [Frederick] Stiffler and [John] Remine were working carrying the men to the bottom of the incline, and there smothering them to death in a massive mountain of snow and broken timbers.*[297]

Unaware that a slide had occurred miners inside made their way to the entrance at shift's end only to discover that the avalanche had sealed the entrance. For three hours they dug before reaching the surface. Destruction met their eyes. The blacksmith shop and their two friends lay unseen under the white mass somewhere down the steep slope. Survivors burrowed two hours before finding the bodies of the hapless victims. Those seeing the slide debris speculated that its size, and the amount of rock and trees carried along, indicated a starting zone very high on the peak and from two separate gulches. It began in one gulch, and when it reached the junction of the second gulch caused it to start sliding.

The Black Bear Mine near Telluride had its tunnel portal located at an altitude of 12,050 feet, much higher than most mines in the country. From March 22 to April 2, 1926, a storm raged over the San Juans. After several days of snowfall a few miners made the decision to ride the tram to town while others stayed at the boardinghouse. They rode in buckets dangling from a cable as the storm pounded and shook their open carriages. Those staying at the mine feared that an avalanche could hit the boardinghouse. After some thought they decided to separate and stay in different areas of the boardinghouse hoping some might be spared to dig out the others.

Black Bear Mine owners had considered the possibility of avalanche danger by building the boardinghouse away from obvious slide chutes. They thought the cliffs above the boardinghouse added extra protection from avalanches as snowslides were channeled safely into gulches on either side. The three-story building accommodated 150 people. The company constructed it with heavy timber anchored by cables into solid rock. Its steeply pitched roof easily shed snow, and it was hoped that the same would be done to an avalanche if one came that way.

From its start in March and into April the snowstorm filled gulches and loaded a large basin high overhead. Loading of new snow on old hard-crusted pack created unstable conditions. The mass reached a point where cohesion was lost and movement began. As it started, a smaller neighboring slide was set in motion. These slides usually ran separately, but this time they came together. The avalanches started at two o'clock in the morning, April 2, 1926. When the mass hit the cliffs the avalanche went right over instead of dividing. Thousands of tons of snow hit the Black Bear Mine boardinghouse and sliced it in half. Half of the building remained in place while the other section splintered into pieces coming to rest a half mile down the mountain.

Two lucky men crept out of the standing portion and searched hastily for survivors following a zigzag pattern. They found and freed the foreman buried to his neck in snow, but unable to move. Karhu, the Shepherd dog, survived but lost his sight and hearing. Another man chipped his way out because a cave had formed around his bunk giving him oxygen and room to move. After several hours of searching the survivors sent a plea for help to Telluride. The blacksmith and his wife remained missing. Over a period of four days searchers probed until they found a green strand of yarn and followed it to the couple's bodies. The blacksmith's wife had been knitting when the avalanche struck.[298]

The Black Bear Mine continued operating after this disaster. Extra precautions were taken to protect the miners.

Near the Gordon-Tiger Mine in 1929 at Twin Lakes two men worked the White Star Mine on the south side of Parry Peak. Every day one of the men would go out of the mine to gather some firewood from a stump above the mine. On this day Jim Foutch hit the stump with an axe and the snow began sliding. Charles Foxall heard the slide from inside the tunnel and ran out to see what happened. He searched the immediate area and found one of Foutch's gloves. He yelled and probed the snow with a stick. Finding no more evidence of Foutch he went for help. The rescuers found Foutch still alive but suffering from multiple injuries. He died nearly a year later from his injuries.[299]

Avalanche danger threatened the children at Camp Bird. One time a slide destroyed the first Camp Bird schoolhouse and was subsequently named the Schoolhouse Slide. Fortunately the schoolhouse was empty at the time. They moved the school next to the Pates Slide on Pates Peak. It:

> . . . was a regular country school with one long narrow room. At one time, it had been a saloon. It was located on this side of Pates Peak . . . right next to the Pates Slide. . . One day I heard the slide start. It sounded like kind of a dull boom. . . . I told the children to cover their faces and get under their desks. That slide divided just above us and roared by on either side. The room filled with a fine snow and mist. . . . I think we all went home early.[300]

The teacher telling this story worked and lived near Camp Bird Mine near Ouray, Colorado, in 1929. His words described the danger experienced throughout this region. He went on to say that the family he lived with near the school and Revenue Mine cabled their house to the rock cliffs. Their home survived snow loading, extremely high winds, and avalanches.[301]

Fifteen miles southwest of Lake City on Henson Creek, the Empire Chief Mine showed renewed promise after a rich vein was discovered in the workings. Owners refurbished old structures and built new buildings including a bunkhouse. Henson Creek near Lake City has a procession of slides with the names Klondike, Big Casino, Copper Gulch, Big Twin, Galena, Sunshine Mountain, Boulder, Wager, Horseshoe, and Gravel. In late March 1929 nearly all had come down. The Copper Gulch Slide left debris fifty feet deep and eight hundred feet long and Big Casino deposited a mass fifteen feet deep and five hundred feet long. These slides destroyed three miles of power line that served Empire Chief Mine.

Buildings at Empire Chief, especially the boardinghouse, were located at seemingly safe places. At about two o'clock in the morning a slide began a mile above the creek bed, but on the opposite hillside from Empire Chief Mine on Gravel Mountain. Billowing snow descended at breakneck speed, hit the valley floor, flowed over a county road and drove three hundred feet up the mountainside engulfing the mine. It buried the boardinghouse under eleven feet of debris.

Many more might have been killed. On the second floor of the boardinghouse nine men slept and nearby so did the three cooks above the main kitchen. The slide sheared off the lower level leaving the second floor lying on top of the avalanche. Richard Halpin was eating lunch in the kitchen and was thrown thirty feet but survived uninjured. Ten men worked in the mine a mile away and soon joined the search. J. J. Strayer was found after searchers heard his calls. A table had overturned lodging in such a way as to protect him from being crushed. Eric Anderson and others were soon found but were frostbitten. Keith Cutting and H. E. Johnson were asleep in the office and did not survive and neither did L. A. Coler and W. I. Wickersham in the bunkhouse. Strayer and Anderson were quickly removed to Lake City for medical care.

In spite of the loss of life, plans went forward to continue developing Empire Chief Mine. The mill located a few hundred yards away stood untouched. The boardinghouse, other buildings, and power line were to be rebuilt and the workforce rehired.[302]

In another heavy snow year during the winter of 1936, ten years after the tragic Black Bear avalanche, heavy snowfall wreaked havoc all over Colorado. Drifts and avalanches blocked roads to mines and tunnel openings almost causing the Arkansas Valley Smelter near

*Trench where a body was found at the Empire Chief avalanche in
1929. Body is above. (Grant Houston Collection, Lake City)*

Taking body of Empire Chief avalanche victim to Lake City for burial. (Grant Houston Collection, Lake City)

Leadville to stop production for lack of ore shipments. The road from Leadville to the Climax Mine over Fremont Pass suffered closure by an avalanche. It isolated Leadville from supplies and the ability to ship ore causing an economic drain on the community. The central mountains were still an area of great mining activity and roads needed clearing for miners to reach the mines. For this purpose a federal rotary plow was assigned for the highway between Leadville and Climax. At this time skiing was becoming a favorite winter sport, and the Denver Mountain Parks developed and owned Winter Park west of the Continental Divide over Berthoud Pass. The storm dumped snow throughout the mountains, but before the plow completely cleared the road to Climax it was moved to clear Berthoud Pass for skiers. That skiers received such priority sent a clear message that the recreation industry had surpassed mining as an economic base of the state. Mining had opened the wilderness by creating the extensive road and trail system that existed at the time. Now the recreation industry directly benefited. Loss of the rotary stranded miners at the mine or in their homes and caused an economic hardship in the mining community. Meetings between angry miners and state transportation officials showed that the tourist industry was favored over mining.[303] The miners' protests caught the ear of the governor who ordered the transportation department to bring in heavy equipment to Leadville and clear the roads. After clearing Berthoud Pass they even brought back the rotary.[304]

This winter was a big snow year for Colorado like the year of the "Big Snow" of 1898-1899, when it had snowed almost continually for six weeks. Railroads and highways that had been blocked four decades before, but not since, once again lay under drifts and avalanches. Transportation over Fremont Pass and Tennessee Pass, and at the old Shoshone Slide in Glenwood Canyon was stalled. Roads and railroads were barricaded and closed by avalanches.[305] Only time would tell what the toll in lost lives and destroyed property would be.

Ben Hartley arrived in Mancos, a community at the extreme southwest edge of the La Plata Mountains between Durango and Cortez, after a desperate dash for help to save people caught by an avalanche at the Hesperus Mine — also known as Doyle Mine — fifteen miles to the northeast. Hartley made his trip on a pair of broken skis, the least damaged of all the skis and snowshoes on hand after the slide had settled. Hartley described some of his ordeal: "When I left camp a strong wind was blowing and heavy snow was falling . . . In a short time I ran into a thick fog which made it impossible to see more than thirty or forty feet."[306]

Sliding, falling, slipping into precipices, climbing out of gulches, and flying over cornices, which suddenly appeared before he could

take evasive action, Hartley pursued his mission. He set off at least
seven avalanches on his harrowing trip. Weary from the trip Hartley
finally attained the valley floor where warming sunshine and the safety
of the town rewarded his efforts. He limped into town on his broken
skis and immediately came under the care and concern of Mancos citizens. They immediately formed a search party.

The Hesperus was located thirty years before by James Doyle.
Investors had recently revived the mine after miners made an important gold strike at nearby Red Arrow Mine in 1933. Usually mines in
the area closed for the long and difficult winters of the southern San
Juans. Hesperus continued operating, employing several miners, mill
workers, and a cook. Over a period of several days snow fell almost
continually. It blocked motor traffic and railroads. Telephone lines lay
broken on the ground. Snow was seven feet deep on the level. Great
drifts formed in gullies from winds that reached twenty or more miles
an hour. Hesperus Mine owners anticipated occasional winter closings
and had supplied the crew with emergency fuel and extra foodstuffs,
and skis and snowshoes in case drifts obstructed the road. At the
Hesperus regular mining activities went on, but many worried pri-
vately that there might be an avalanche. To avoid tempting fate the
supervisor shut the mill down. Rumbling vibrations from heavy
machinery might jar loose the already unstable snowpack.

Its site at an altitude of 11,000 feet exposed the Hesperus Mine to
severe winter weather. Jackson Ridge towered more than a thousand
feet over the mine and buildings. The ridge was named in honor of
George A. Jackson who discovered the first important gold strike in
Colorado near Idaho Springs. It is a mountain structure that can be
described as a perfect basin for collecting large amounts of snow. It is
long and curves gently from southwest to northeast entirely above timberline. Just above the mine is a cliff that runs the entire length of the
lower slope of Jackson Ridge. Almost directly above the mine portal is
a break in the cliffs where the spring melt gushes through like a water-
fall. This break in the continuity of the cliff provided a funnel for thousands of tons of snow to drop directly onto the mine and buildings. On
that tragic day a fracture appeared close to the ridge top. Hesitating for
a moment it then spread horizontally completing a tear across the
entire width of the basin.[307] From that fracture line and below, thousands of tons of snow moved slowly and then gathered speed. Cohesion
of snow on the slope completely failed and the slide gathered mass and
strength signaling its life with a boom. In a fast descent of over a mile,
rock, brush, and trees were gathered up contributing to the slide's
ability to deliver a death-dealing blow. Funneling through the break in
the cliff the mass hit full force and destroyed the substantial mill,
bunkhouse, cookshack, storehouse, and other buildings leaving only

broken posts sticking up to indicate where habitation and industry had existed. This had happened before. While the discoverer of the mine, James Doyle, ran the mine in years past a slide came down and destroyed a building in the same place as the 1936 avalanche.

After the avalanche slowed and stopped, survivors looked across the debris in horror. They saw only rocks, timber and splintered milled lumber. After collecting themselves, they joined together to probe, search, and dig for missing people. The avalanche blew Mrs. Rees and Miss McCaleb from the floor of the cookshack up to the rafters. Mrs. Rees died from injuries, but Miss McCaleb clung to the rafters and survived. Survivors found several others alive in the wreckage.

The avalanche swept away or destroyed most of the skis and snowshoes provided by the owners. The carpenter tried to repair a pair of skis or snowshoes so that someone could go for help. By Monday morning he partially repaired a set of skis and Ben Hartley slid out on his dash for help. The fifteen survivors set up temporary quarters in the food storage shelter and the part of the mill not swept away. They found a few blankets, fuel and food.

Moments after Hartley reached Mancos, the townspeople phoned news of the disaster to Durango and Cortez. Highway crews began clearing the road from Cortez to Mancos so that more rescuers could assist in the effort. Tractors and a plow started the laborious task of opening the road to the Hesperus Mine. By Tuesday they had only opened it to within six miles of the mine. From the end of the plowed section, Sheriff Robinson and forty searchers skied or snowshoed the remaining distance as heavy snow and zero degree temperatures settled in over the La Plata Mountains.[308]

The search continued over several days. Long trenches were dug in an attempt to intersect bodies. Little hope was held out that anyone buried could have survived, but searching continued until five of those who perished were found. Parley Jensen's body turned up only after April temperatures melted away his snowy tomb.

The avalanche extensively damaged all buildings at Hesperus Mine.[309] Earl Wyman, Charles Rossier, Clint Noble, Roy McGuire, Parley Jensen and the cook, Mrs. Jane Rees died.[310]

The same storm that lead to tragedy at Hesperus created conditions for avalanching at Camp Bird Mine near Ouray. The avalanche at Camp Bird came down the Chicago Cliff and thundered a mile and a half along the Devil's Slide path striking first the property known as the King Lease operated by Charles Bell and Joe King. Charles's son, Franklin Bell, Colorado School of Mines student Frank Read, and forty-five men had been working the mine throughout the winter.[311] The King Lease was mining the upper workings of Camp Bird properties. The slide then continued on to Camp Bird Mill, tore through the camp and ripped a hole through a bunkhouse leaving the building in place, but disturbing several sleeping miners on the second floor. Debris completely covered the mill and took the pump house away. The avalanche continued to run for another mile without causing further damage or injury. The fifteen miners asleep in the bunkhouse were not hurt. In a gulch nearby a second slide ran and might have caused even greater destruction if a heavy timber avalanche wall had not been in place. When the snow settled three people lay dead in the debris. After it settled the avalanche measured one and a half miles wide and up to twenty feet deep.

First reports of the 1936 Camp Bird Slide gave a fatality count of nine. Avalanches had earlier taken out telephone poles severing communication. Friends and relatives in town could not ascertain the true conditions at the mine. Snow depths amounted to eight feet on the level and snow continued falling. Rescue parties rode on horseback from Ouray to relieve the suffering of the stranded or injured. The avalanche sealed the tunnel entrance trapping twenty-five miners. After digging for twelve hours with miners' picks and shovels they saw light and escaped through a snow tunnel twenty-five feet long.[312] The camp cook Rose Israel, mill foreman Chapp E. Wood, and mine blacksmith Ralph Klinger were killed. Rose Israel had gone outside the bunkhouse to watch the avalanche when she heard it start. It swept her away.[313] Chapp Wood, the mill superintendent, drowned in the pump house when snow filled the room and the weight forced his head under water in the tank he had attended. With great effort they found the bodies of Mrs. Israel and Ralph Klinger in debris far below the mine. James Dunn, the mine superintendent, survived trapped in the bunkhouse until rescued.[314] Forty survivors prudently evacuated the area bringing the three who died to Ouray three days later when better conditions made for safer travel.[315]

The deadly slide at Camp Bird was nearly equaled on April 1 when The Bankers' National Mine boardinghouse was swept down the mountain one evening. Never before had a slide passed at that location. They constructed the buildings where it seemed safe. Erin Higginbotham survived and made his way to Camp Bird for help. A search party found George Rabb's and John Orth's bodies. Several miners on their shift in the tunnel escaped unharmed.[316]

In the high mountains, snow and avalanches are constantly reclaiming the works of man. Flattened buildings at high altitudes result from heavy snow loading and avalanches. In 1941 newspapers noted that avalanches were reclaiming many mines in the San Juans during a heavy year of sliding. On Red Mountain several slides covered mine shafts and tunnels with debris, and leveled numerous buildings. After being untouched for many decades the Iowa Mill in Arrastra

Gulch with its heavily constructed buildings and massive equipment was demolished by a slide. The Old Hundred Mine was struck around the same time with some property damage.[317] Five years later a huge avalanche buried dozens of shafts and destroyed property on Red Mountain. This seemed to mark the end of a mining era that had started more than seventy years earlier.[318] Here people had scratched out a living from minerals buried deep in the mountains. A place that in decades before had lived with constant dynamite blasting, the shrill and clatter of trains pulling up steep grades, and the yells of muleskinners fell to silence. The avalanches came down returning humanity's work to earth's ancient and natural ruggedness.

East Schoolhouse slide on the road to the Camp Bird Mine. On February 14, 1958, three men were killed in this slide. In this photo the vehicle seen at center was covered. The crew who shot this slide for safety reasons had to walk back to town. (Ouray County Historical Museum, Ouray, Colorado)

On February 14, 1958, Ted Mason and Harry Peck had to walk from Ouray to Camp Bird Mine since the county road was blocked by more than two feet of new snow. As they reached the West Waterhole Slide path an avalanche descended. Peck yelled to Mason and ran but Mason failed to respond and became entombed in the massive slide. After a fruitless search Mason went on to Camp Bird for help. Four men responded. Superintendent Walt Smith, Danny Jerrell, Joe

Martinez and Mike Muransky arrived at the scene with two bulldozers. Near the scene of the first slide one of the bulldozers broke down and three of the men gathered to investigate. Then the East Schoolhouse Slide ran burying the men and the caterpillar. Joe Martinez was hurled through the air but landed in soft snow unhurt. Other searchers arrived and long poles were used to probe for the victims. Under eighteen feet of snow the bulldozer was reached but no sign of the men could be found. Temperatures remained low and new snow fell imperiling searchers. The next day searching continued but on Sunday warming temperatures created high danger and the search was called off. On Tuesday a howitzer was brought in and the slopes stabilized by shooting several shells into the paths overhead. A week passed since the first slide before all bodies were uncovered.[319]

The town of Twin Lakes grew up at the base of Colorado's highest peak, Mt. Elbert. It lies at the base of the south extension of Mount Elbert called Parry Peak. While placer and lode mining existed in nearby gulches, Twin Lakes was actually a resort community for the silver kings from Leadville and their investors. The producing mines on Parry peak included the White Star Mine and Gordon-Tiger Mine. Giant avalanche runs are well defined on Parry Peak and these have destroyed property and taken life on several occasions. The first time was in 1899, then in 1916 and again in 1929. Backcountry skiers and mountaineers have suffered death at the hands of avalanches over many decades on Mount Elbert.

In the early winter months of 1961-1962 there were fatalities of skiers and mountaineers at the north end Mount Elbert. Later that winter, just west of Twin Lakes, one of the most deadly slides in recent memory visited. There were signs that avalanche conditions had reached critical levels. Along the highway and on hillsides snow sloughed off and higher up avalanches could be seen running. The highway that runs through Twin Lakes was a route blazed by pioneers and is a favorite road for tourists to travel in the summertime to Aspen over Independence Pass.[320] The weather conditions of the winter of 1961-62 created textbook avalanche conditions. Heavy early season snowfall followed by warm temperatures generated an icy crust on top of unconsolidated depth hoar crystals at the bottom of the snowpack. Little additional snow fell until the third week of January when a strong storm front moved in and dumped up to forty inches of snow on the mountains. On January 21 snow fell heavily at Twin Lakes and wind rearranged snow on the peaks that loaded starting zones and filled gulches. Twin Lakes had remained a resort area since the heyday of mining so most people who lived there in the summer had returned to their permanent residences elsewhere in the country. A half mile west of Twin Lakes seven families stayed on throughout the winter.[321]

High on Parry Peak at about the 13,000-foot level, snowpack strained under the weight of so much extra snowfall and wind loading. A Chinook wind blew and probably added to the instability of the snowpack. Then there was a shudder and a large crack formed near the top of the ridge. The crack zipped horizontally across the snowpack and thousands of tons of snow began falling.

> *No one knows what triggered the slide. . . . Far up, in the darkness before dawn, snow came down two chutes, joined, and in seconds the whole mountain seemed falling. Directly in the path, lay the Gordon Mine, an abandoned gold digging with heavy timbered buildings, a power plant, and a locomotive-size steam boiler. . . .*[322]

Avalanche paths on Parry Peak that joined in 1962 to produce the deadly Twin Lakes disaster. At bottom of photo, left of center, is the lateral moraine that usually contained avalanches before they reached the settlement. (J. W. Jenkins Photo)

Then in the gully just to the west another avalanche started at about the same time. The avalanches reached speeds up to 130 miles per hour and joined where the gullies came together. This gave the slide tremendous power. It achieved an unforgiving and unstoppable momentum. Air pressure created in front pushed buildings of the Gordon Mine off their foundations before the mass of snow hit. Then the avalanche front struck and finished ripping the heavily-timbered buildings from the earth. It lifted the power plant and its locomotive-size steam boiler and floated them along like toys. Within seconds the avalanche dropped into a 300-foot deep lateral moraine left over from the action of glaciers thousands of years ago. The ravine created by the moraine usually stopped the forward progress of slides, preventing a run to the valley floor. This time the mass filled the gully then popped over the top to continue its death-dealing flight into the valley flats where it " . . . came on like a hurricane toward the houses . . .. "[323] The avalanche cut telephone and electrical wires at Twin Lakes leaving clock hands pointing at 5:31 in the morning. People living in and around Twin Lakes had given some thought to the possibility of a slide coming that way but dismissed the possibility of real damage or injury. William Adamich had such thoughts but a huge rock stood above his house and he believed this would split an avalanche causing it to flow around the house harmlessly.

Upper limit of one of the slide paths that resulted in the Twin Lakes disaster of 1962. Thousands of tons of snow were left behind running only a short distance. (Colorado Historical Society)

When the avalanches began the village of Twin Lakes was still asleep, and before daylight the slide arrived on the valley floor. General Shelton, wife Marle, and their children Steve, Linda, and Vickie seemed secure in their home. The Adamich family slept nearby in their home. Arising at four in the morning to let the dog out Adamich noticed the unusually heavy snow that accumulated overnight.[324] Returning to bed Mr. Adamich heard nothing unusual and neither did anyone else as tons of snow began careening down the mountainside. The weight and force of the snow uprooted trees and carried along splintered debris from the Gordon Mine. Finally it met the valley floor and spread out over several acres. The giant boiler came to rest just above Highway 82 where it remains to this day. Not a soul heard or saw the avalanche start, run, or settle. Nils Lindstone awoke well after light and looked at his clock that still showed 5:31. The electricity must have gone out during the night he thought — an occasional occurrence in this rural community. Glancing at his wristwatch he noted the time to be 7:30. He looked outside and saw that his driveway had been plowed the night before by his neighbor General Shelton. Then at about 8:30 in the morning Nils heard a knock at the door and when he opened it saw the ashen face and excited voice of friend Jack Rowe. It was then that Nils stepped out and saw the edge of the avalanche and a scene of:

> *. . . a house trailer . . . on top of a tilted house next door. Adamich's barn was gone, along with a garage and other buildings. There was no trace of Adamich's house or the Sheltons' [house]. Where there had been a forest, the mountain was bare. . .*[325]

Jack Rowe ran the half mile to Twin Lakes to find a working phone and call for help. Lindstone started to collect tools for searchers as soon as they arrived. Rowe returned as quickly as he left and breathlessly said that the phones were all down and they needed a car to drive to Granite to call for help. The men went to the home of Climax miner Bud Davis since his car was the nearest one that looked like it could be dug out. The snowplow the night before had packed snow tightly against the car and while the men worked a car with two skiers pulled up on the way for a day of skiing. When they saw the slide and the trouble the men were having freeing the car they immediately volunteered to turn around and drive back to Granite. They contacted highway worker Paul Poplin who then called the sheriff's office. The skiers returned to Twin Lakes to help in any way possible.

The Rinker family owned a lodge four miles up the road from Twin Lakes and became fearful during the night that a slide might hit their home. They decided to leave for a safer place. As they drove toward Twin Lakes they encountered a small slide blocking the road and had to leave the car and begin walking the remaining distance to Twin Lakes. Then they came across the huge slide covering the highway. The

Rinkers immediately joined in the search effort, and while the group debated on what to do Bob Rinker pointed to a rise in the usually flat area of a nearby meadow and asked, "What's that?" They rushed to the spot and recognized the structure as Adamich's house that had been moved 500 feet from its foundation. The rock that Adamich thought would save his family had been broken into rubble. They heard a moan and found William Adamich lying halfway out of the house.

House moved from its foundation by the 1962 Twin Lakes ava-lanche. (Colorado Historical Society)

By this time the Leadville radio station had broadcast the news and people from Twin Lakes and towns all around Lake and Chaffee Counties began to arrive with jack hammers, crow bars, shovels, axes, and every imaginable tool to search for the unfortunate victims. Soon soldiers from the Tenth Mountain Division arrived with tracked vehicles and knowledge of mountain search and rescue. Lake County Search and Rescue and volunteers from the Sheriff's department, ski areas, other rescue teams, and individuals came until nearly 500 searchers combed every inch of the debris area. In two or three hours hundreds of people assembled for searching and hundreds more spectators clogged the highway for nearly four miles east of Twin Lakes.[326]

The avalanche's destructive work horrified those at the scene. The Sheltons' home was five hundred feet away from its foundation and lay in pieces. The Adamich house, along with another house, cabin, garage, and dairy barn with seventy-five cows were gone. Several vehicles including three trucks, two pickups, two tractors, two trailers, and machinery lay scattered and broken. The road disappeared for nearly a thousand feet. The six-ton boiler from Gordon-Tiger Mine was in view on top of the snow after traveling nearly two miles.[327]

Searchers formed long probe lines and used compressed air hoses to thrust jets of air in the debris to break up the mass.[328] Mrs. Adamich was the second survivor found at eleven that morning after being buried for nearly six hours.[329] William Adamich spoke of his ordeal when he:

> *. . . awoke suddenly and heard a loud crack like the house had blown up. The house started moving and then caved in and snow came into my face. A dresser and two sliding closet doors came across the room and fell over me forming a kind of lean-to. When the snow and debris stopped moving, I was pinned in a twisted, almost standing position . . .*[330]

Probe line searching for victims of the Twin Lakes avalanche. (Colorado Historical Society)

Tenth Mountain Division from Camp Hale removing a tree from the 1962 Twin Lakes avalanche that killed seven. (Colorado Historical Society)

Searchers found others throughout the day, but none survived. They uncovered fifteen-year-old Steve Shelton at one in the afternoon, and soon after, his parents. Bodies of the two Shelton daughters Linda and Vickie were found embracing each other indicating they heard the slide and had time to reach each other. On January 22 the rescue continued but no other victims could be located. The next day a 75-mm howitzer was brought in to shoot down potentially dangerous slides threatening the searchers. While a few small slides ran the remaining snowpack seemed to hold. Finally on January 23 the Adamich children, Mike and Billy, were found.[331] Of the nine caught, only Mr. and Mrs. Adamich survived.[332]

Twin Lakes is in view, but was not directly hit by the Twin Lakes avalanche in 1962. The actual damage was at homes a half-mile west of the town. The lateral moraine at center left usually stopped snow slides but the extra heavy snowfall and the joining of the two slides and then running together overwhelmed the moraine and the avalanche ran to the valley. (J. W. Jenkins Photo)

Survivors of the slide William and Barbara Adamich received the warmest support from Leadville residents. A fund was set up at Climax Mine to receive donations for the Adamichs who had lost not only their children, but all that they owned including a home and dairy business. The little dog Pepe who also survived was pregnant at the time. The puppies were auctioned off bringing $6,600 dollars to the family. William Adamich was given his old job back at Climax Mine. The Adamiches never lived at Twin Lakes again. Another sad result of this avalanche monster was the death of William Adamich's mother a few weeks later. She apparently died from the stress and shock of losing her grandchildren.[333]

Statistics show the power of this avalanche. It is described as a climax avalanche which means, in this case, that the entire snowpack slid down to the surface of the ground. It started at 12,000 feet on Parry Peak and dropped 3,000 vertical feet over a path 9,000 feet in length. Along its run, two more avalanche paths were undercut and added to the mass. Near the bottom a glacial moraine about a hundred feet high usually acted as a barrier to stop the progress of slides in this active avalanche path. This time the slide exploded over the barrier and continued to the valley floor 1200 feet below.[334]

The scene of this disaster can be viewed about one half mile west of the western end of Twin Lakes. The boiler, partly crushed, is just above the highway on the north side of the road. The hillside north of the highway is barren and strewn with debris carried from mine structures thousands of feet above the lake. Evidence of the foundation of the dairy barn is in the runout zone south of the highway.

Boiler from the Gorden Mine thousands of feet above on Parry Peak on the Twin Lakes avalanche. The boiler is the size of a small truck and rode on the surface the entire trip of nearly two miles. The boiler is in view a few feet above Highway 82 the summer road to Aspen from Denver. (J. W. Jenkins Photo)

Many active avalanche paths threaten Colorado mountain passes throughout the snow season including Monarch Pass, Wolf Creek Pass, Berthoud Pass, and most of all Red Mountain Pass. Red Mountain Pass has always presented danger to travelers going to camps like Ironton, Red Mountain, or Silverton. The "Million Dollar Highway" passes through and under no less than sixty-three active avalanche paths, which may run during or after every storm, in its twenty-three mile course between Ouray and Silverton.[335]

When first constructed in the last quarter of the nineteenth century, the roadbed ran lower in the canyon than the present route. Avalanches slammed into the gorge depositing debris many tens of feet deep and hundreds of feet long throughout the winter. When too deep for a cut to allow passage, tunnels were driven large enough for a stagecoach and team to pass. These tunnels sometimes extended 600 feet in length with thirty or more feet of icy mass overhead. They often lasted until the spring melt. Snow tunnels became unnecessary after the road was rerouted higher on the rocky canyon wall since slides tend to hit the highway and then continue to the floor of the gulch leaving much less debris to be cleared with a snowplow.[336] One particularly troublesome slide area is the East Riverside Slide and West Riverside Slide on opposite sides of the highway about five miles south of Ouray. The East Riverside has a catchment basin of 75 acres; the West has twice that amount. The East Riverside descends a path of nearly 3,200 vertical feet; the West runs about the same distance. At the last moment of its descent, the East Riverside Slide is channeled into a narrow gulch before hitting full force on the roadbed and continuing to the Uncompahgre River. The West Riverside is of similar force, but encounters the riverbed first where much of its energy is dissipated. Occasionally these slides run simultaneously.

The Colorado Highway Department received its first 75 mm howitzer from the National Guard in 1953. In Utah the howitzers proved effective after being put into service after World War II.[337]

On March 3, 1963, a storm of normal proportions for the San Juans raged. Reverend Marvin Hudson who served the towns of Ouray and Silverton set out with his two daughters, Amelia and Pauline, for Silverton early that Sunday morning despite pleading by his congregation to avoid the crossing. The road had been closed several times during the night from constant avalanching. Several snowplows operated through the night and managed to open the road for short periods of time, but soon another slide would come and cover the road. The Reverend was accustomed to this process and determined to cross over Red Mountain Pass to conduct services. He had previous experience with avalanches. Two years before a slide ran and blocked his way. Another motorist stuck on the other side walked across and the men exchanged cars and continued on to their respective destinations.

On this morning the minister and his daughters approached the East Riverside Slide that had just run but was being cleared. Plows had cleared a path wide enough for a single car. As he entered the slide area the car lost traction and spun out. Reverend Hudson stopped his car to put on chains while still in the slide path, probably believing that all the snow had already been stripped from the slopes above. As he was putting chains on his car the East Riverside Slide struck again announcing its presence by surcharging the air with powdery snow. One snowplow was hit and pushed into the other. When the air cleared and the slide settled the Reverend, his daughters, and the car had disappeared.

On the second day of searching for Reverend Hudson and his two daughters neither they nor the car had been found. It would be a week before the Reverend was found and spring when the last daughter's body was recovered. (Ouray Historical Society)

A search immediately began as other motorists who saw the event piled out of their cars with shovels. A radio call brought in twenty more searchers, and a hasty search and rough probing got under way but without success. The search persisted into the evening under conditions of blowing snow and sub-zero temperatures. The canyon below held the debris of the Reverend's car and the bodies of himself and daughters in a depth up to sixty feet.

Monument on Red Mountain Pass for Reverend Marvin Hudson and his daughters, Amelia and Pauline, killed in 1963 at the East Riverside Slide south of Ouray, Colorado. (Denny Hogan Photo, Colorado Avalanche Information Center)

The search continued Monday with fifty searchers, metal detectors, and dogs, but yielded nothing. On the third day bulldozers were brought in to strip away large areas and then probe lines were formed to search the area cleared. Even psychic techniques such as divining and witching sticks were pressed into service in this desperate undertaking. Danger from above remained high so a howitzer was brought in to shoot the avalanche paths and stabilize the snowpack. For seven days the searching continued before Reverend Hudson's body was discovered. Three days later one of the daughters was found, but not for three months was her sister's body recovered. It is believed that all died instantly, as the force and tonnage of the slide so violently whisked away the car, leaving it mangled, with Reverend Hudson swept away and the two sisters thrown from the vehicle.[338]

One of the lessons of this tragedy is that although an avalanche has run once there is no guarantee that the sliding has ended. In this case sufficient snowpack remained to fuel another deadly avalanche.

The site of this avalanche tragedy is on US 550 south of Ouray. Just past the East Riverside snowshed is a turnout with a memorial to the three who died. Nearby is another monument to the snowplow drivers who have lost their lives trying to keep the road open over the past several decades.

CHAPTER 8

❄

Recreation and Avalanches

> *A meteorologist in 1910 noted: "It was not only the quantity of snow that fell that caused so many avalanches, but also the manner in which it fell." — United States Forest Service, Snow Avalanches,* A Handbook of Forecasting and Control Measures.[339]

Now as in the past, avalanches threaten those seeking recreation and adventure. For most of the twentieth century fewer casualties from avalanches have been counted, but the possibility of loss of life remains. The roads pioneered by miners over a hundred years ago have been improved making travel to ski areas and backcountry recreation areas easier. Where miners faced White Death daily in order to sustain a living, people seeking recreation go by choice. It is easy to fall into a belief that large-scale avalanche disasters that destroy property and cause multiple deaths are in the past. It is clear that as the new rush for "white gold" continues there is a marked increase in the average yearly fatality toll of people pursuing recreation in the high mountains. Technology has been both a blessing and a curse. It has helped to reduce the number of fatalities by the invention and widespread use of avalanche beacons which can speed rescue efforts by a victim's companions. But technology has increased danger by making it possible for people to travel easily to high mountain areas where they are exposed to avalanches. Lightweight ski equipment, snowmobiles, helicopter skiing, and other means of transport make access to remote areas easier. Persons seeking thrills and fun can easily reach places that put them in harm's way. Resorts are at a greater risk as housing and lodge construction fills valley floors and gulches. This implicit danger became reality in the death of six-year-old Terry Huddleston in February of 1989, when an avalanche swept over the parking lot of a condominium at Crested Butte where he and his family were staying.[340]

Four highways in Colorado have the distinction of claiming the most highway and recreational avalanche victims. In the San Juans, Highway 550 from Ouray to Silverton is the most avalanche-prone road in the country. Slides often run during and soon after a storm and less predictably at other times. The other highways are U.S. 40 over Berthoud Pass, U.S. 6 over Loveland Pass, both of which are west of Denver, and Wolf Creek Pass in Southwestern Colorado. Wolf Creek Pass is nearly as dangerous as Red Mountain Pass, but a snowshed and other structures combined with occasional road closures lower the danger to motorists. Berthoud Pass has claimed many lives resulting from the many cirques and conditions that create avalanches and its easy access near a large population center. Loveland Pass is similar to Berthoud Pass being close to an area with a large population and easy to reach. These four highways have over 300 places where avalanches may run.[341]

Skiing today is a high-tech industry with composite skis made of a variety of natural and manufactured materials. Ski length, stiffness, and other properties are tailored to meet the ability and use of the individual. Early skis were wood and of various widths and lengths up to twelve or more feet long. Instead of poles for assistance in fast, precise turning, early skiers used a long pole that served as a rudder and for balance. Skis were called "snowshoes," and snowshoes, "webs." Ski clubs existed at several mining camps, notably Nevadaville near Central City and at Crested Butte.

The first recorded recreation-related death by avalanche was near Silverton at the Irene Mine in February 1905. Two miners, trying out their new production skis, left their cabin to ski an inviting slope. Another man watched from the cabin. As the skiers started they set off a slide that had its origin far above the skiers. It carried them only thirty feet but both perished before they were found.[342]

Skiing became important in the 1930s. Even at this early date two men were claimed at the Berthoud Pass Ski area on February 7, 1937. Their bodies remained hidden until spring. On April 1, 1949, seventeen-year-old Sidney Prather died in an avalanche at Loveland Basin ski area. By 1957 skiing's importance was recognized when a skier appeared on Colorado license plates. On April 8 of the same year, one of the most famous and talked about avalanche disasters happened on the route to Denver Mountain Parks' ski resort of Winter Park on the western side of Berthoud Pass.

The story begins when Roland Wyatt, eighteen years of age, and twenty-six-year-old freelance photographer John Hermann left Salt Lake City on a vacation. Along the way Hermann received word from Disney Studios that he had been awarded a contract to film a documentary on avalanches. The men changed their plans and decided to travel to locations known for avalanche activity. First they traveled to Colorado's most active avalanche region, the San Juan Mountains, in the southwest. After spending a few days traveling around the area, particularly along the highly avalanche-prone Million Dollar Highway the pair found little activity. They drove to Berthoud Pass where avalanche shoot-downs commonly took place to protect skiers and other traffic over the pass. The men arrived the first week of April 1957 and inquired at the highway department about the possibility of a shootdown so they could film a slide in motion. The most likely candidate was the Dam Slide, threatening U.S. 40, three miles west of the community of Empire on Blue Creek Mountain. State highway department worker Ted Bakken, after much hounding by the photographer, agreed to shoot the avalanche on Monday April 8, 1957. It was an effort that was to take place anyway during the week to make the road safe for the expected heavy weekend ski traffic.[343] During the first week of April seventy-nine inches of snow fell fueled by an upslope weather system. Winds averaged twenty or more miles an hour for over four days. Often avalanches run in their paths when heavily loaded, but the Dam Slide held precariously to Blue Creek Mountain. The Dam Slide had never reached the road since 1933 and usually stopped in a run-out zone before reaching the highway.[344]

Early Monday afternoon the 75-mm howitzer was placed in position for the shoot. Roland Wyatt set a camera in a remote location to the side of the avalanche path, and connected a 200-foot-long cord that was used to start the camera rolling from a remote and safe location. John Hermann placed his camera on the highway directly below the avalanche path, next to his station wagon, and remained there waiting for the shoot. Highway department worker Wayne Whitlock stood at the west end of the slide boundary by his state truck to stop traffic. The slide was not expected to run to the highway. The three man howitzer team started by lobbing a first, then second shell, onto the avalanche path without a shiver from the snowpack. They loaded a third, took careful aim and shot. The mass quaked, shuddered, and moved. It descended in seconds. Thousands of tons of snow were brought down. All were surprised at the size of the monster and its speed, allowing little time for those below to take cover. The slide moved " . . . silently at first, then jumped the 100-yard wide bed of Clear Creek. It boiled up more than ten feet onto the road in a tidal wave of white that covered 700 feet of highway ten to twelve feet deep."[345]

Within seconds an estimated 600,000 tons of snow fell to the highway completely entombing Hermann and Whitlock and catching Wyatt as he tried to retreat into the trees away from the path. Hermann saw that the slide would soon be upon them and yelled to his companion to get out of the way. The tons of snow were preceded by a thousand foot plume of powdery snow spiraling overhead.[346] Wyatt told of his experience as he:

> *. . . ran for the trees. I was within four feet of safety when the avalanche hit me like a shock wave, lifting me ten feet in the air. . . . I could see trees falling 'round me. Then I was smacked over on my face, under the snow. My arms over my face gave me a little breathing space, and I dug — the wrong way at first. But, after a minute I clawed free — the snow was about two feet deep over me. I staggered about and looked back at the highway.*[347]

What he saw was the White Death spreading across the highway and into Clear Creek below, with no sign of his friend, the station wagon, or the highway worker and his truck.

The leader of the shoot team, Ted Bakken, described how the avalanche hesitated, gathering snow for about three minutes before gaining speed. The slide fell into Clear Creek, but then jumped the high embankment and flowed onto the road. After the avalanche settled motorists watching the disaster piled out of their cars with shovels to begin a frantic search for victims. Rescuers with probe poles and a mine detector came in and began the tedious search.[348] Whitlock's body was found that evening by the probe pole team. Hermann's body was discovered in the early hours of Tuesday " . . . encased in a wall of marble-like snow, frozen in a running position with a large log jammed against his back."[349]

This event was one of the most famous avalanche tragedies. The camera placed at the base of the slide path continued rolling until completely enveloped by the slide. It showed dramatically the relentless power of a huge avalanche and the helplessness of anyone caught in its grip.

Governor McNichols ordered an immediate investigation into the fatal accident. Blame and finger-pointing began with Ted Bakken, shoot team leader, saying that area supervisor Pat Murray had given the go ahead. Murray said that Bakken had told him the men had been hounding him for days to go ahead with the shoot. Murray stated that Bakken said he could trigger the slide, but had not been informed prior to the event. In shoot-downs where the public is not at risk the shoot team can work without higher-level permission. The Dam Slide was not expected to run to the highway. Chief Highway Engineer Mark Watrous knew the slide would be shot, but gave no formal permission. Unofficial sanction was given to control the Dam Slide and another area on Loveland Pass, but a schedule was not set.[350]

After investigation by Governor McNichols into the causes and responsibility of those involved in this tragedy, guidelines were drawn up for highway workers on protecting the public from being injured or killed during the dangerous business of avalanche control.

At the time of the shoot, avalanche expert Dr. Maximillian Schantl, Director General of the Austrian Federal Railways, was sightseeing on Loveland Pass. The tragedy encouraged Dr. Schantl to comment on avalanche control in Austria where railroads, highways and population are at greater risk. He said Colorado would benefit and save money by building avalanche control structures. In Austria permanent systems of earth or stone pyramids, retaining walls, snowsheds, and snow fences slow, break up, stop or redirect snow away from roads, railroads, and homes. Snow fences placed high on peaks near ridge summits stop the formation of or hold back cornices. Pyramids break up running avalanches into less damaging streams. Retaining walls stop or hold back snow from running while snowsheds guide the avalanche harmlessly over highways. These structures are very expensive to build, but once in place can protect life and lessen damage to property.[351] Colorado has some of these structures along Red Mountain Pass and Wolf Creek Pass.

Throughout the next two decades, avalanche fatalities showed a steady increase but were usually less than four per year. Then in 1987 eleven died in several incidents. All involved people pursuing recreation, mostly skiers, and all were out-of-bounds at ski areas or in the backcountry. The next deadliest year, previous to 1987, was 1906 when twenty died in the San Juans and many more in other locations in Colorado. The avalanche deaths in 1906 were at mining camps or were mining related. One difference between the two years is that in 1906 slides were not always triggered by those caught. In 1987 all of the fatalities were triggered by people who were caught.[352] Statistics since 1970 revealed the continuing upward climb of fatalities in recreation-related avalanche deaths. From 1970 to 1980, thirty persons were caught and three killed. In the two seasons of 1984 through 1986, eighty-three were caught, with eight fatalities. In the winter season of 1986-1987, fifty-nine were caught and eleven perished.[353] This statistic has not been matched since that year, but the trend of higher average yearly fatalities continues. From 1987-1988 to 1993 a total of thirty-six fatalities, an average of six deaths per year, were recorded.[354] Four of these fatalities occurred near one of Colorado's most popular ski resorts — Breckenridge.

At the Telluride ski mountain in the snowy and rugged San Juan Mountains of southern Colorado, avalanche conditions reached a peak. The Telluride ski area was opened in the early 1970s and gained a reputation similar to Aspen, of being a home to cultural and artistic events. Each year Telluride hosts music, art, and movie festivals, balloon races, and ultra-marathon runs. The narrow valley drained by the San Miguel River is somewhat isolated with its glaciated and steep rocky ranges on three sides with an opening to the north. After the 1893 demonetization of silver, gold and the base metals of zinc, copper, and lead kept mining going into the 1970s. Finally, mining succumbed to market forces of cheaper production overseas.

Yet Telluride lives on. "White gold" replaces the shiny metals and attracts tourism, land development, and investment to the region. The tremendous snowfall of the San Juan range was a bane to many economic ventures, but it is a boon to skiing and backcountry activities. Telluride is recognized as one of the world's premier ski areas and is becoming a renowned cultural center.

At Telluride, Bear Creek Canyon claimed several lives in the 1986-1987 season. Each of the victims made mistakes from which lessons may be learned. In the first incident on January 8, Garrett Gravalli of Taos was cross-country skiing with four other companions when he was caught and killed. The five had some backcountry experience and decided to cross an area evaluated as possibly dangerous. The party correctly decided on a strategy to cross one at a time while the others remained in a safe location and watched. After the first skier successfully crossed, Gravalli became impatient and started across and was carried to his death. This experience points to the unpredictability of avalanche stability. Gravalli probably assumed that since a slide did not occur when the first person crossed then the snow must be stable.

On the second day of February several skiers were skiing in the same area where Gravalli died. Again the group started by being cautious and sending one skier across at a time. The first skier pushed off, but before he made it the other side, the others became impatient and followed. The resulting slide buried and killed Brett Perry and Michael Walliskey. They made the same mistake as the earlier party. Perry had even taken the wise precaution of calling the Colorado Avalanche Information Center before leaving on the excursion and learned of high avalanche danger in the Telluride backcountry, but the skiers decided to continue with their plans, with tragic results.

In mid-March two snowmobilers died on Shrine Pass. The conditions were similar to those at Breckenridge with old snowpack being covered and weighted by new heavy snowfall. The snowmobilers crossed a particularly unstable area setting off the slide that killed them.[355]

Two weeks before the Shrine Pass avalanche a former ski patrolman died on Wolf Creek Pass in southwestern Colorado. Russell Forster died of injuries when a slide smashed him into a tree. Forster and companions were skiing Treasure Mountain when the slide started. The others watched from a safe location while Forster went for a second run. Sheriff Phillip Leggitt stated, "It caught him in the middle (of the slope) and wrapped him around a tree. Ninety inches of snow were on the ground and the top thirty-four inches made the avalanche." All had operating avalanche beacons. When the slide came to rest Forster's companions began a search and found him in just ten minutes under two feet of snow. The men were well trained in emergency medicine and tried to revive Forster over a period of two hours. The odds for survival in this slide were high for Forster. His friends were well trained, had watched his run from a safe distance, noted where he went under and quickly started a search. If his injuries had been less severe Forster might have survived.[356]

The experienced and informed skier knows the risks he or she takes and should be responsible for his/her actions. On the other hand, someone with little or no experience is an unfortunate victim when caught. Dr. Douglas Fields skied out-of-bounds with several friends when a slide took him over a cliff to his death. Fields was new to skiing and had little experience in mountain safety. It was the lack of knowledge that killed him.[357]

The tragedy of these avalanches is clear and the causes are easily assessed. Except for Dr. Fields, all of the victims knew the odds and had some experience evaluating the danger. The slides all happened outside of ski area boundaries and were set off by those caught. These four separate tragedies were overshadowed by a single slide near Breckenridge ski area. It is the single deadliest recreation-related avalanche disaster in Colorado.

It was during the unusually high snowfall year of 1986-1987 that this avalanche disaster transpired. The slide was in an out-of-bounds area near the Breckenridge ski area. It was a classic example of avalanche danger formation when old snowpack had reformed with a covering of crust, or ice, from thawing and freezing over a period of two months of dry and warm weather. Heavy February storms laid fresh layers of snow over the hard surface of old snow. The avalanche near the Breckenridge ski area was not the first of the season. The fresh powder called out to skiers and adventurers, and huge numbers overwhelmed the mountains everywhere in Colorado.[358]

The 1986-1987 ski season began with early heavy snowfall kicking off what appeared to be a good start. Then a snow drought settled in and very little snowfall made it to the central Rockies. Temperatures moderated, creating a hard crusty snow surface and unconsolidated temperature gradient layer up to eighteen inches thick near ground level. A slick surface and unstable lower snowpack waited for new and adequate snowfall. The storm arrived in the middle of February dumping from seven to fourteen inches of snow. Skiers came out in droves. Ski resorts recorded some of the highest attendance ever.[359]

At Breckenridge ski area skiers packed the slopes after the storm laid down fresh powder several inches deep. On Peak Seven, an out-of-bounds area but accessible by a gate with a warning sign, several skiers had crossed from ski area boundaries into the uncontrolled avalanche area. A trail was there for skiers to cross from one ski hill to another although it was clearly in an avalanche area. Most skiers followed the trail from one hill to the other without incident, two climbed higher up to ski the mostly untracked powder in this semi-wilderness. Two weeks before, a pair of skiers were caught in the same area but both dug out without injury. While dangerous, there were no legalities in place that could bring charges to anyone skiing this out-of-bounds hill since it was on Forest Service lands and therefore open to all. Skiers were discouraged to enter by a sign stating the clear and present danger.

> *If you are injured in any way or are buried by an avalanche while skiing the backcountry, be reminded that rescue by the Summit County Sheriff's Office may be slow and costly.*

During high use times Breckenridge Ski Company posted a ski patrolman at the gate to monitor and further warn and discourage skiers from leaving the avalanche-controlled ski area. No skier had ever been seriously injured or killed by an avalanche within the boundaries of Breckenridge ski area.

Sign warning skiers of the grave danger when entering the out of bounds area of Breckenridge ski area. In 1987 Peak Seven was not part of the ski area but being on Forest Service was open to general use. (Nick and Mary Logan, Colorado Avalanche Information Center)

On this mostly sunny day several skiers followed the trail from one hill to the other. Two skiers, Rick Gale and Tom Castrigno, climbed to the top of Peak Seven to ski the steep, wide, and powdery expanse. When the men reached the top they prepared to make the run. They were experienced skiers and equipped for the possibility of an avalanche. Avalanche beacons were set to transmit and shovels were ready in their backpacks. The two waited at the top of the hill until they could see no skiers below. But out of sight, three skiers sat on the snow while a fourth looked for a lost ski. Castrigno skied off first then pulled to the side to what seemed like a safe place to wait. Gale followed and also stopped in a safe area. As he stood there assessing his next route he heard yelling and saw the mountain begin to move starting at a point 150 feet above. Then it released under his skis, but being near the edge of the slide, he managed to ski to the side and safety.[360] A 1,600 foot long fracture line appeared and a slab covering several acres ran 1,120 vertical feet. The crown, or headwall, of the fracture was three to five feet in height. When it stopped, and settled, the deposition area covered almost twenty-four acres.[361] Gale watched to see if anyone would be buried and after the slide stopped he saw an arm " . . . sticking out of the snow waving frantically."[362] Gale skied to the partially-buried victim and with his shovel quickly dug him out. Tim Kirkland, who had been waiting while his companion searched for a ski, was safe but the others were caught.[363] While gasping for air the buried skier survived. Gale stayed until night ended rescue efforts. That first day rescuers arrived within minutes lead by Breckenridge ski area ski patrollers Mary Logan, Kevin Ahern, and Paul Miller. Ahern contacted the Summit County Sheriff and local rescue teams were notified. Within an hour over eighty volunteers assembled and joined the grim search. Using probe poles, and beacons, the volunteers searched debris ten to twenty-five feet deep. As night fell one of the victims was found dead in addition to the rescue made by Gale when the slide occurred earlier that day. By the end of the day estimates of the missing reached five or six, but one fact was sure — this would be the

Skiers viewing the search area below. The fracture line was a quarter mile in length and the headwall from three to five feet in height. (Nick and Mary Logan, Colorado Avalanche Information Center)

worst ski accident in Colorado history in an already record year for recreation-related avalanche deaths.[364] Breckenridge ski resort suffered cancellations, and inaccurate reports in the world press stated up to 200 deaths in the event.[365]

Probe line at the debris area of the 1987 avalanche. (Nick and Mary Logan, Colorado Avalanche Information Center)

As dawn broke over the high peaks on the second day, February 19, a helicopter flew along the ridges, and dropped explosive charges to stabilize dangerous snowpack before searchers arrived. On this day dogs and teams locally, and from around the state, joined the effort.[366] Summit County Search and Rescue and ski patrols from Copper, Arapaho, Vail and others arrived along with mountain rescue teams. Alpine Rescue Team showed up with nearly two-dozen members, but Rocky Mountain Rescue stayed in reserve to respond to the likely possibility of rescues elsewhere in Colorado. Skiers riding lifts gave up their day and volunteered to help. Up to 200 searchers lined the search area on the second day. On that day the bodies of New Zealanders Paul Way and Nicholas Casey were pulled from the wreckage. Housemate Ian McQuarrie fell to his knees and wept at the loss of his longtime ski friends.[367]

On the third and last day of the search an estimated three hundred volunteers showed up to continue the effort. Avalanche dogs continued working, but their usefulness may have been compromised by contamination of so many searchers during the previous day. George Cates was skiing with his half-brother, seventeen-year-old Alex Cates, when the avalanche started. George's recollections of the scene pointed to where his brother went under and led searchers to the body. The snow was packed hard as concrete around young Alex. George expressed tremendous guilt for bringing his brother, who was half his age, into the out-of-bounds area.

The ensuing investigation by Sheriff Delbert Ewoldt discovered that Rick Gale and Tom Castrigno might have set off the slide. No charges were filed because all the skiers were on Forest Service land. Both men suspected of starting the slide responded immediately when the slide stopped to search for victims. Gale was responsible for saving one victim. The men came forward and told their stories to authorities immediately and admitted to being high on Peak Seven at almost 12,000 feet. While the men had been cautious, they could not account for all the skiers below when the avalanche fell. Gale said in an interview that he would carry guilt for the rest of his life. The result of this tragedy has brought some changes in Summit County on how to handle skiers in out-of-

Before the searchers resumed the search on the second day charges were dropped from the helicopter on suspected unstable snow pack. (Nick and Mary Logan, Colorado Avalanche Information Center)

bound areas. Under the Colorado Ski Safety Act of 1979 ski areas can fine skiers who cross boundary ropes if the ski area has leased or plans to develop the area being entered. The act also allows authorities to restrict or stop rescues in backcountry areas if avalanche danger is high. Those rescued may be charged for the cost of rescues that can amount to tens or hundreds of thousands of dollars. As a result of this accident, the Summit County Sheriff's Office can issue citations to skiers caught crossing boundary ropes or skiing into closed areas. These fines can amount to hundreds of dollars.

Avalanche Search dog, Hasty, indicating a possible find of a victim of the 1987 Breckenridge avalanche. While dogs are the best hope for finding avalanche victims they were brought in too late for this effort. Contaminated by rescuers and snowmobiles made discerning the scent of those buried too difficult for the dogs. (Nick and Mary Logan, Colorado Avalanche Information Center)

Skiers and backcountry travelers can help lower their chances of death and injury by education and clear thinking. Education should be directed at gaining knowledge and skills in avalanche danger recognition and rescue. Mountain clubs, outdoor recreation stores, mountaineering guides, and others offer courses. Clubs and guides can be found in the phone book, advertised in mountaineering stores and announced in newspapers. There may be a small cost but it is worth every penny. The course should explain mountain weather, snow dynamics, and how avalanche danger evolves. The course should have a field day where a trip to the peaks is required for studying snowpack and assessing weather. Use of avalanche beacons should be taught and practiced. A list of minimum equipment for survival and rescue should be given. After that it is up to you. Travel in Colorado's backcountry is especially dangerous in winter. Risk always exists winter and summer. Have in a pack the ten essentials of a map, compass, flashlight/headlamp, extra food, extra clothing, sunglasses, first aid supplies, pocketknife, matches, and fire starter. Purchase, maintain and use an avalanche beacon. Each member in the party must have one, and set to transmit. Each member must carry a shovel. Follow travel and slope crossing rules taught in class. If someone is caught, note where the person went under. Change all beacons to receive and begin a search as taught in avalanche class. All members of the party should remain at the search area. Be sure to assess further avalanche danger and keep another tragedy from happening. This brief outline does not come close to giving the knowledge necessary for safe backcountry travel. Only classes and experience will fulfill the requirement.

Hauling a victim of the Peak Seven avalanche disaster of 1987. (Nick and Mary Logan, Colorado Avalanche Information Center)

For all the danger posed by avalanches the lure of the wild is irresistible. Enjoy the wild and all that it does for the human spirit but be knowledgeable, thoughtful, and act defensively. Remember that you are the visitor to the wilderness and must adjust to that environment. Enjoy your stay and make it possible to visit again.

A. A. Lamont wrote a poem titled *On San Juan Hills* as a memorial to the many lives lost to avalanches in the San Juan Mountains. He speaks to all who have perished in an avalanche or have been among the survivors:

Our San Juan hills beneath the snowdrifts lying,
In cold embrace life's fitful dream now o'er;
In darkened homes in sorrow bowed and sighing,
Loved ones are left to weep upon Time's shore.

On San Juan hills they freely toiled to lighten
Exacting wants which ever to men come;
The hearts now full of gloom how oft did lighten
When labor's fruit came to the dear old home.

On San Juan hills their gold was purchased dearly,
For complex life has never-ending needs;
And all who work for food and drink see clearly
That sweetened life is kept by helpful deeds.

On San Juan hills we all can learn life's lesson;
To improve the moments as they swiftly go.
The avalanche of death perhaps hangs o'er us,
And may come as swiftly as the sliding snow.

On San Juan hills in bloom of youth cut early
From loving and from loved ones here below;
And from all the things they prized on earth most dearly,
On San Juan hills lie buried 'neath the snow.[368]

INDEX

BIBLIOGRAPHY
BOOKS

Aldrich, John K. *Ghosts of Chaffee County.* Lakewood: Centennial Graphics, 1989.

Aldrich, John K. *Ghosts of Lake County.* Lakewood: Centennial Graphics, 1986.

Aldrich, John K. *Ghosts of Pitkin County.* Lakewood: Centennial Graphics, 1987.

Aldrich, John K. *Ghosts of the Eastern San Juans.* Lakewood: Centennial Graphics, 1987.

Aldrich, John K. *Ghosts of the Western San Juans,* Vol I. Lakewood: Centennial Graphics, 1988.

Armstrong, Betsy R. And Williams, Knox. *The Avalanche Book.* Golden: Fulcrum Publishing. 1992.

Athearn, Robert G. *The Denver and Rio Grande Railroad.* Lincoln: University of Nebraska Press, 1962.

Bancroft, Caroline. *Colorado's Lost Gold Mines and Buried Treasure.* Boulder: Johnson Publishing Company, 1961.

Bancroft, Caroline, *Tabor's Matchless Mine and Lusty Leadville.* Boulder: Johnson Publishing Co., 1960, 1960.

Benham, Jack L. *Camp Bird and the Revenue.* Ouray: Bear Creek Publishing Company, 1980.

Brown, Robert L. *Ghost Towns of the Colorado Rockies.* Caldwell: Caxton Printers, Ltd., 1990.

Campbell, Rosemae Wells. *Crystal River Valley.* Denver: Sage Books, 1966.

Corregan, Robert A. and Lingane, David F. *Colorado Mining Directory, 1883.* Denver: The Colorado Mining Directory, 1883.

Crofutt, George A. *Crofutt's Grip-Sack Guide of Colorado.* Omaha: The Overland Press Co., 1885.

Crossen, Forest. *Western Yesterdays.* Vol. I. Boulder: Paddock Publishing, Inc., 1966.

Crum, Josie Moore. *Ouray County Colorado.* Hamilton, Illinois: Hamilton Press, Inc., nd.

Crum, Josie Moore. *The Rio Grande Southern Railroad.* Durango: Hamilton Press, Inc., 1961.

Crum, Josie Moore. *Rails Among the Peak.* St. Paul: Railroader Printing House, 1956.

Dallas, Sandra. *Colorado Ghost Towns and Mining Camps.* Norman: University of Oklahoma Press, 1985.

Digerness, David S. *The Mineral Belt.* II. Silverton: Sundance Publications, Ltd., 1978.

Digerness, David S. *The Mineral Belt,* Vol. III. Silverton: Sundance Publications, Ltd., 1982.

Dyer, Reverend John L. *The Snow-Shoe Itinerant.* Cincinnati: Cranston & Stowe, 1890.

Eberhart, Perry. *Guide to the Colorado Ghost Towns and Mining Camps.* Chicago: The Swallow Press Inc., 1959.

Ferrell, Mallory Hope. *Silver San Juan.* Boulder: Pruett Publishing Company, 1973.

Foote, Mary Hallock. *A Victorian Gentlewoman in the Far West.* San Marino: The Huntington Library, 1972.

Fraser, Colin. *Avalanches and Snow Safety.* New York: Charles Scribner's Sons, 1978.

Gardiner, Charles Fox, M.D. *Doctor at Timberline.* Caldwell: The Caxton Printers, Ltd., 1939.

Griswold, Don and Griswold, Jean. *Colorado's Century of "Cities."* No Publisher. Copyright 1958 by Don and Jean Griswold and Fred M. and Jo Muzzula.

Hafen, Leroy R. and Hafen Ann. *The Colorado Story.* Denver: The Old West Publishing Company, 1953.

Hauck, Cornelius W., Chappell, Gordon and Richardson, Robert W. *The South Park Line, A Concise History.* Colorado Rail Annual No. 12. Golden: Colorado Railroad Museum, 1974.

Helmers, Dow. *Historic Alpine Tunnel.* Chicago: Sage Books, The Swallow Press, Inc., 1963.

Hill, Emma Shepard, ed. *Foundation Stones.* Denver: The Bradford Robinson Printing Co., 1926.

Hunt, Inez and Draper, Wanetta W. *To Colorado's Restless Ghosts.* Denver: Sage Books, 1960.

Ingersoll, Ernest. *The Crest of the Continent.* Glorieta, New Mexico: The Rio Grande Press, Inc., 1969.

Jocknick, Sidney. *Early Days on the Western Slope of Colorado.* Glorieta, New Mexico: The Rio Grande Press, 1968.

Lathrop, Gilbert A. *Little Engines and Big Men.* Caldwell: Caxton Printers, Ltd., 1954.

Lavender, David. *The Rockies.* New York: Harper & Row Publishers, Inc., 1968.

Logan, Mary. *Article of the Breckenridge Avalanche Disaster in 1987.* Breckenridge: Colorado Avalanche Information Center, 1987.

Marshall, John and Roberts, Jerry. *Living (and dying) In Avalanche Country.* Silverton: A Simpler Way Book Co., 1992.

Ormes, Robert M. *Tracking Ghost Railroads In Colorado.* Colorado Springs: Century One Press, 1975.

Pearce, Sarah J., and Eflin, Roxanne. *Guide to Historic Aspen and the Roaring Fork Valley.* Evergreen: Cordillera Press, Inc., 1990.

Poor, M. C. *Denver, South Park and Pacific.* Denver: Rocky Mountain Railroad Club, 1976.

Schader, Conrad F. *Colorado's Alluring Tin Cup.* Golden: Regio Alta Publications, 1992.

Setnicka, Tim J. *Wilderness Search and Rescue.* Boston: Appalachian Mountain Club, 1980.

Sharp, Verna. *A History of Montezuma, Sts. John, and Argentine.* Dillon: Summit Historical Society, 1971.

Shoemaker, Len. *Roaring Fork Valley.* Silverton: Sundance Publications, Ltd., 1958.

Simmons, Virginia McConnell. *Bayou Salado: The Story of South Park.* Colorado Springs: Century One Press, 1966.

Simmons, Virginia McConnell. *The Upper Arkansas.* Boulder: Pruett Publishing Company, 1990.

Sloan, Robert E. *The Rainbow Route.* Denver: Sundance Publications Limited, 1975.

Stevenson, Thelma V. *Historic Hahn's Peak.* Fort Collins: Robinson Press, Inc., 1976.

Stoehr, C. Eric. *Bonanza Victorian.* Albuquerque: University of New Mexico Press, 1975.

Stone, Irving. *Men to Match My Mountains.* Garden City: Doubleday & Company, Inc., 1956.

Ubbelohde, Carl; Benson, Maxine; and Smith Duane A. *A Colorado History.* Boulder: Pruett Publishing Company, 1972.

Williams, Knox and Armstrong, Betsy. *The Snowy Torrents, Avalanche Accidents in the United States, 1972-79.* Jackson: Teton Bookshop Publishing Company, nd, (c. 1985).

Wolle, Muriel Sibell. *Stampede to Timberline.* Chicago: Sage Books, The Swallow Press, Inc., 1949.

NEWSPAPERS

Aspen Times. 1881-1899.

Aspen Democrat. 1882-1906.

Carbonate Chronicle. 1916-1968.

Carbonate Chronicle. Griswold, Don and Griswold, Jean, "The Homestake Tragedy." January 22, 1968: 8 and January 29, 1968: 8.

Chaffee County Times. 1884.

Colorado Graphic. 1888.

Colorado Transcript. 1893-1914.

Colorado Republican. 1862.

Daily Transcript. 1875.

Denver Post. 1892-1995

Denver Post. Farrell, John Aloysius. "Das Lautier." *Contemporary Magazine.* March 9, 1986, 17 & 31.

Denver Post. Adamich, Barbara. "Avalanche!" *Contemporary Magazine.* April 15, 1962: 10-11, 24.

Denver Post. Scher, Zeke. "Avalanche: Colorado's White Death." *Empire Magazine.* December 1, 1974: 47-54.

Denver Republican. April 1, 1893, 1.

Denver Times. April 12, 1900, 1.

Denver Tribune Republican. 1883-1885.

Georgetown Courier. 1916.

Greeley Tribune. 1875-1877.

Gunnison Review Press. 1883-1899.

Gunnison News Champion. 1885-1893.

Lake City Times. 1906.

La Plata Miner. 1882-1902.

Leadville Herald Democrat. Lindstone, Nels G. February 10, 1967.

Leadville-Herald Democrat. 1879-1936.

Moly News. 1962.

184 ❋ BIBLIOGRAPHY

Pueblo Chieftain. February 16, 1969.
Rocky Mountain News. Foster, Jack. "Homestake Avalanche." January 24, 1962: 35.
Rocky Mountain News. 1859-1995.
Rocky Mountain News. Kelly, George. "That Night on Homestake Mountain." *Rocky Mountain Empire Magazine.* July 4, 1948: 5.
Silver World, 1878-1990.
Salida Record. 1883-1914.
Silverton Standard. 1906.
Solid Muldoon. 1883.
Summit County Journal. 1884-1899.
The Weekly News. March 6, 1878.
White Pine Cone. 1881-1893.

PERIODICALS
Denver Westerners Roundup. Vol XIV, No. 2, February 1958.
Fales, Jr., E. D. "Terror at Twin Lakes." *Popular Science.* Vol 182, February 1963: 114-117.

GOVERNMENT PUBLICATIONS
United States Forest Service. *Snow Avalanches a Handbook of Forecasting and Control Measures.* FSH2. USDA, Washington: US Government Printing Office, 1961.
Berry, J. W. *Climatological Summary, 1931-1960.* Climatography of the United States, No. 20-5. US Dept. of Commerce, nd.
Frutiger, Hans. *Snow Avalanches Along Colorado Mountain Highways.* Rocky Mountain Forest and Range Experiment Station. Fort Collins: US Forest Service, July 1964.
Gallegher, Dale, ed. *The Snowy Torrents. Avalanche Accidents in the United States, 1910-1966.* Alta: US Forest Service, Alta Avalanche Center, 1967.
Mehls, Steven F. *The Valley of Opportunity. A History of West-Central Colorado.* Lakewood: Bureau of Land Management, Colorado State Office, 1988.
Perla, Ronald I., and Martinelli, Jr., M.. *Avalanche Handbook.* Fort Collins: USDA, Forest Service, 1976.

INTERVIEWS
Interview. Betsy Stitzer. Gunnison, Colorado. 18 October 1973.
Interview. Margaret and Raleigh Flick. Ohio City, Colorado. 23 January 1974.
Interview. Nick Logan, Colorado Avalanche Information Center, Boulder, Colorado. January, 2000.

MANUSCRIPT
Logan, Mary. Report of the 1987 Breckenridge Peak Seven Avalanche. Breckenridge, 1987.

COLLECTIONS
Grant Houston Collection, Lake City, 1996 (photos, articles, research materials, manuscripts).

Randall Clippings. Denver Public Library, Western History Department. Vol. 2, p.269, January 1916.

Root Collection. Colorado State Historical Society.

PHOTOGRAPH COLLECTIONS

Colorado Railroad Museum, Golden, Colorado.

Colorado State Historical Society, Denver, Colorado.

Denny Hogan, Buena Vista, Colorado.

Denver Public Library, Western History Department, Denver, Colorado.

Grant Houston Collection, Lake City, Colorado.

Lake County Public Library, Colorado Mountain History Collection.

Nick and Mary Logan, Colorado Avalanche Information Center, 1987 Avalanche, Breckenridge Colorado.

Ouray County Historical Society, Ouray, Colorado.

San Juan County Historical Society, Silverton, Colorado.

ENDNOTES

1 Colin Fraser, *Avalanches and Snow Safety,* (New York: Charles Scribner's Sons, 1978): 5.

2 Fraser, 10.

3 Fraser, 12.

4 Fraser, 18.

5 Fraser, 19.

6 Fraser, 19.

7 Fraser, 20.

8 Fraser, 79.

9 Fraser, 22

10 US Department of Agriculture, Forest Service, *Snow Avalanches, A Handbook of Forecasting and Control Measures* (FSH2, 2332.81, Washington, 1961): 4-5.

11 US Department of Agriculture, Forest Service, *Snow Avalanches, A Handbook of Forecasting and Control Measures* (FSH2, 2332.81, Washington1961): 4.

12 David Lavender, *The Rockies* (New York: Harper & Row Publishers, Inc., 1968): 361.

13 Ronald I. Perla, and M. Martinelli, Jr., *Avalanche Handbook* (Fort Collins: USDA Forest Service, 1976): 3-4.

14 Charles Fox Gardiner, MD, *Doctor at Timberline* (Caldwell, Idaho: The Caxton Printers, Ltd., 1938): 20.

15 Knox Williams and Betsy Armstrong, *The Snowy Torrents. Avalanche Accidents in the United States* (1972-79, (Jackson, Wyoming: Teton Bookshop Publishing Company, N.D.): 212.

16 Ernest Ingersoll, *The Crest of the Continent,* (Glorietta, New Mexico: The Rio Grande Press, Inc., 1969): 145.

17 Sandra Dallas, *Colorado Ghost Towns and Mining Camps* (Norman: University of Oklahoma Press, 1985): 101.

18 *Rocky Mountain News,* March 6, 1861, 1.

19 *Colorado Republican,* April 10, 1862, 1.

20 *Colorado Republican,* April 10, 1862, 1.

21 Caroline Bancroft, *Colorado's Lost Gold Mines and Buried Treasure* (Boulder: Johnson Publishing Company, 1961) 18.

22 Sandra Dallas, *Colorado Ghost Towns and Mining Camps* (Norman: University of Oklahoma Press, 1985): 174.

23 Verna Sharp, *A History of Montezuma, Sts. John, and Argentine* (Dillon, Colorado: Summit Historical Society, 1971): 16.

24 Sharp, 20.

25 Dallas, 133.

26 *Weekly Rocky Mountain News,* March 4, 1874, 1.

27 *Greeley Tribune,* April 14, 1875.

28 *Denver Daily Tribune,* February 18, 1879.

29 *Greeley Tribune,* April 21, 1875.

30 *Daily Transcript,* March 27, 1875, 1.

31 *Weekly Rocky Mountain News,* April 28, 1875, 4.

32 Gardiner, 44.

33 *Greeley Tribune,* January 17, 1877, 1.

34 *Greeley Tribune,* January 17, 1877, 1.

35 Robert E. Sloan, *The Rainbow Route* (Denver: Sundance Publications Limited, 1975): 15.

36 Inez Hunt and Wanetta W. Draper, *To Colorado's Restless Ghosts* (Denver: Sage Books, 1960): 319.

[37] Don Griswold and Jean Griswold, *Colorado's Century of "Cities"* (n..p., Copyright by Don and Jean Griswold, and Fred M. and Jo Muzzula, 1958): 120.
[38] John K. Aldrich, *Ghosts of the Western San Juans, Vol. I* (Lakewood: Centennial Graphics, 1988): 25.
[39] *Silver World,* February 23, 1878, 3.
[40] *Silver World,* February 23, 1878, 2.
[41] *Silver World,* January 4, 1879, 3.
[42] Muriel Sibell Wolle, *Stampede to Timberline* (Chicago: Sage Books, The Swallow Press, Inc., 1949): 257.
[43] Wolle, 257.
[44] Wolle, 257-258.
[45] Bancroft, *Colorado's Lost Gold Mines and Buried Treasure,* 15.
[46] Wolle, 258.
[47] Bancroft, *Colorado's Lost Gold Mines and Buried Treasure,* 15.
[48] Wolle, 258.
[49] Ingersoll, 143.
[50] John K. Aldrich, *Ghosts of the Western San Juans, Vol. I.* (Lakewood: Centennial Graphics, 1988): 9.
[51] *Silver World,* March 2, 1878, 2.
[52] *Silver World,* March 1, 1879, 3.
[53] *Silver World,* March 23, 1878, 2.
[54] *Silver World,* March 30, 1978, 3.
[55] *Ouray Times,* June 29, 1878, 3.
[56] *Silver World,* February 22, 1879, 3.
[57] *Ouray Times,* February 15, 1879, 3.
[58] *Denver Tribune,* February 10, 1881, 1.
[59] Quote on exhibit at the Ouray Historical Museum of J. T. Pierson, 1940.
[60] Sarah J. Pearce and Roxanne Eflin, *Guide to Historic Aspen and the Roaring Fork Valley,* (Evergreen: Cordillera Press, Inc., 1990): 41.
[61] Dallas, 16.
[62] Pearce and Eflin, 41.
[63] *Leadville Herald-Democrat,* March 14, 1884, 1.
[64] *Aspen Times,* March 22, 1884, 1.
[65] *Aspen Times,* March 22, 1884, 1.
[66] *Aspen Times,* March 22, 1884, 1.
[67] *Aspen Times,* March 14, 1885, 1.
[68] *Pueblo Chieftain,* February 16, 1969, 7D, c 1-4.
[69] Dallas, 145.
[70] *Pueblo Chieftain,* February 16, 1964, 7D, c 1-4.
[71] Dallas, 186.
[72] Jack L. Benham, *Camp Bird and the Revenue,* (Ouray: Bear Creek Publishing Co., 1980): 21.
[73] John K. Aldrich, *Ghosts of the Western San Juans, Vol. I.* (Lakewood: Centennial Graphics, 1988): 42.
[74] *Solid Muldoon,* December 28, 1883, 3.
[75] *Denver Tribune,* December 25, 1883, 1.
[76] Benham, 23.
[77] *Silver World,* January 5, 1884, 3.
[78] *Solid Muldoon,* December 28, 1883, 3.
[79] Sidney Jocknick, *Early Days on the Western Slope of Colorado* (Glorieta, New Mexico: The Rio Grande Press, 1968): 310.
[80] Griswold and Griswold, *Colorado's Century of "Cities,"* 201-204.

[81] Gardiner, 17.

[82] Jocknick, 310.

[83] *Gunnison Daily Review-Press,* January 31, 1883, 1.

[84] Wolle, 212-214.

[85] *Gunnison Daily Review-Press,* January 30, 1883, 1.

[86] *Gunnison Review-Press,* April 1, 1885, 4.

[87] *Gunnison Daily Review-Press,* February 5, 1883, 2.

[88] *Aspen Daily Times,* March 5, 1899, 2.

[89] George A. Crofutt, *Crofutt's Grip-Sack Guide of Colorado,* (Omaha: The Overland Press Co., 1885): 97.

[90] Wolle, 202.

[91] Crofutt, 97.

[92] *Ouray Times,* March 11, 1882, 3.

[93] M. C. Poor, mem. ed., *Denver, South Park and Pacific,* (Denver: Rocky Mountain Railroad Club, 1976): 349.

[94] Poor, 351.

[95] Emma Shepard Hill, ed. *Foundation Stones,* (Denver: The Bradford Robinson Printing Co., 1926): 192-193.

[96] *Chaffee County Times,* March 13, 1884, 1.

[97] Poor, 349.

[98] *Leadville Herald Democrat,* March 12, 1884, 1.

[99] *Leadville Herald Democrat,* March 12, 1884, 1.

[100] Poor, 351.

[101] Dow Helmers, *Historic Alpine Tunnel,* (Chicago: Sage Books, The Swallow Press, Inc., 1963), 45.

[102] Poor, 351.

[103] *Colorado Transcript,* March 19, 1884, 3.

[104] *Colorado Transcript,* March 19, 1884, 3.

[105] Conrad F. Schader, *Colorado's Alluring Tin Cup* (Regio Alta Publications, 1992): 155.

[106] *Summit County Journal,* May 2, 1885, 4.

[107] Caroline Bancroft, *Tabor's Matchless Mine and Lusty Leadville* (Boulder: Johnson Publishing Co., 1960): 187.

[108] Leroy R. Hafen and Ann Hafen, *The Colorado Story* (Denver: The Old West Publishing Company, 1953): 176.

[109] John K. Aldrich, *Ghosts of Lake County* (Lakewood: Centennial Graphics, 1986): 35.

[110] Bancroft, *Tabor's Matchless Mine and Lusty Leadville,* 11.

[111] Mary Hallock Foote, *A Victorian Gentlewoman in the Far West,* (San Marino, CA: The Huntington Library, 1972):

[112] Virginia McConnell Simmons, Bayou Salado, *The Story of South Park* (Colorado Springs: Century One Press, 1966): 145.

[113] *Daily Rocky Mountain News,* December 17, 1879, 3.

[114] *Daily Rocky Mountain News,* December 17, 1879, 3.

[115] *Daily Rocky Mountain News,* December 17, 1879, 3.

[116] *Denver Tribune Republican,* April 27, 1885, 1.

[117] Perry Eberhart, *Guide to the Colorado Ghost Towns and Mining Camps* (Chicago: The Swallow Press, Inc., 1959): 207.

[118] *Denver Tribune Republican,* April 27, 1885, 1.

[119] Griswold, 132.

[120] Eberhart, 208.

[121] *Leadville Herald Democrat,* January 1, 1911, 1.

[122] *Leadville Herald Democrat,* January 1, 1911, 1.

[123] *Leadville Herald Democrat,* January 1, 1911, 1.

124 Kelly, 5.
125 Kelly, 5.
126 Jack Foster, "Homestake Avalanche," *Rocky Mountain News,* January 24, 1962, 35.
127 Kelly, 5.
128 Kelly, 5.
129 *Denver Tribune-Republican,* April 27, 1885, 1.
130 *Denver Tribune-Republican,* April 27, 1885, 1.
131 Don Griswold and Jean Griswold, "The Homestake Tragedy," *Carbonate Chronicle,* January 22, 1968, 8.
132 Don Griswold and Jean Griswold, "The Homestake Tragedy," 8.
133 *Gunnison Review Press,* April 28, 1885, 1.
134 Don Griswold and Jean Griswold, "The Homestake Tragedy," 8.
135 Don Griswold and Jean Griswold, "The Homestake Tragedy," 8.
136 Kelly, 5.
137 Don Griswold and Jean Griswold, "The Homestake Tragedy," 8.
138 Don Griswold and Jean Griswold, "The Homestake Tragedy," 8.
139 Gardiner, 17.
140 *Silver World,* February 13, 1886, 3.
141 *Silver World,* January 15, 1887, 3.
142 *Grant Houston Collection,* Lake City, 1996.
143 *Colorado Graphic,* January 7, 1888, 5.
144 Wolle, 211.
145 *Denver Republican,* March 13, 1891, 1.
146 Josie Moore Crum, *Rails Among the Peaks,* (St. Paul: Railroader Printing House, 1956): 251.
147 David S. Digerness, *The Mineral Belt, Vol. II* (Silverton: Sundance Publications, Ltd., 1978): 373-375.
148 *Denver Post,* January 29, 1899, 6.
149 Dallas, 214-215.
150 *Leadville Herald Democrat,* January 31, 1899, 1.
151 *Leadville Herald Democrat,* January 31, 1899, 1.
152 *Denver Post,* January 30, 1899, 10.
153 Digerness, II,
154 *Denver Post,* March 5, 1899, 20.
155 *Denver Post,* January 31, 1899, 2.
156 *Denver Post,* January 31, 1899, 2
157 *Denver Post,* January 31, 1899, 2.
158 *Denver Post,* January 31, 1899, 2.
159 *Leadville Herald Democrat,* January 31, 1899, 1.
160 *Leadville Herald Democrat,* January 31, 1899, 1.
161 *Leadville Herald Democrat,* January 31, 1899, 1.
162 *Denver Post,* January 30, 1899, 10.
163 *Denver Post,* February 4, 1899, 1.
164 *Leadville Herald Democrat,* February 3, 1899, 1.
165 *Leadville Herald Democrat,* February 3, 1899, 1.
166 *Denver Post,* February 5, 1899Error! Bookmark not defined., 8.
167 *Denver Post,* February 12, 1899, 3.
168 *Denver Post,* February 22, 1899, 1.
169 *Leadville Herald Democrat,* February 2, 1899, 1.
170 *Leadville Herald Democrat,* February 2, 1899, 1.
171 Ernest Ingersoll, *The Crest Of the Continent,* (Glorietta, New Mexico: The Rio Grande Press, Inc., 1969): 376.

[172] *Denver Post,* January 30, 1899, 1.

[173] *Denver Post,* February 2, 1899, 1.

[174] *Denver Post,* February 3, 1899, 1.

[175] *Denver Post,* February 4, 1899, 1.

[176] *Denver Post,* February 11, 1899, 1.

[177] *Denver Post,* February 13, 1899, 1.

[178] *Denver Post,* February 12, 1899, 1.

[179] *Denver Post,* February 13, 1899, 1.

[180] *Leadville Herald Democrat,* February 12, 1899, 1.

[181] *Denver Post,* February 13, 1899, 1.

[182] *Denver Post,* February 22, 1899, 1.

[183] *Denver Post,* March 5, 1899, 1.

[184] Dallas 15.

[185] *Denver Post,* February 22, 1899, 1.

[186] *Denver Post,* February 2, 1899, 1.

[187] *Rocky Mountain News,* March 30, 1899, 1.

[188] John K. Aldrich, *Ghosts of Lake County,* (Lakewood: Centennial Graphics, 1986): 40.

[189] *Denver Post,* February 4, 1899, 1.

[190] *Denver Republican,* March 10, 1899.

[191] Robert L. Brown, *Ghost Towns of the Colorado Rockies,* (Caldwell: Caxton Printers, Ltd., 1990): 229.

[192] John K. Aldrich, *Ghosts of Chaffee County,* (Lakewood: Centennial Graphics, 1987): 42.

[193] *Root Collection,* 1883, (Colorado State Historical Society, 1991): 4.

[194] *Pueblo Chieftain,* February 16, 1969, 7D, C1-4.

[195] *Betsy Stitzer Interview,* Gunnison, Colorado, 18 October 1973.

[196] *Margaret and Raleigh Flick Interview,* Gunnison, Colorado, 23 January 1974.

[197] *Leadville Herald Democrat,* March 21, 1899, 8.

[198] *Leadville Herald Democrat,* March 21, 1899, 8.

[199] *Leadville Herald Democrat,* March 29, 1899, 1.

[200] *Rocky Mountain News,* January 31, 1899, 1.

[201] *Denver Post,* January 30, 1899, 1.

[202] *Denver Post,* February 5, 1899, 8.

[203] *Colorado Transcript,* February 15, 1899, 9.

[204] *Leadville Herald Democrat,* February 12, 1899, 1.

[205] *Rocky Mountain News,* February 16, 1947.

[206] *Georgetown Courier,* January 15, 1916.

[207] *Denver Post,* February 22, 1899, 1.

[208] *Denver Republican,* February 23, 1899, 1.

[209] *Denver Republican,* November 13, 1899

[210] Schader, 177.

[211] *Denver Times,* March 1, 1902.

[212] *The Weekly News,* March 6, 1878, 2.

[213] Irving Stone, *Men to Match My Mountains,* (Garden City: Doubleday & Company, Inc., 1956) 356.

[214] Ingersoll, 129.

[215] Carl Ubbelohde, Maxine Benson and Duane A. Smith, *A Colorado History,* (Boulder: Pruett Publishing Co., 1972): 175.

[216] Mallory Hope Ferrell, *Silver San Juan,* (Boulder: Pruett Publishing Company, 1973) 264.

[217] John K. Aldrich, *Ghosts of the Western San Juans, Vol. I,* (Lakewood: Centennial Graphics, 1988): 36.

[218] *Aspen Democrat,* March 21, 1906, 1.

[219] Aldrich, *Ghosts of the Western San Juans,* Vol. I, 15.

[220] Aldrich, *Ghosts of the Western San Juans,* Vol. I. 15.

[221] *Denver Post,* February 24, 1936, 3.

[222] Jack L. Benham, *Camp Bird and the Revenue,* (Ouray: Bear Creek Publishing Co., 1980) 45.

[223] C. Eric Stoehr, *Bonanza Victorian,* (Albuquerque: University of New Mexico Press, 1975) 144.

[224] Josie Moore Crum, *Ouray County Colorado,* (Hamilton: Hamilton Press, Inc., n.d.): 74.

[225] Wolle, 408.

[226] *Denver Post,* February 17, 1958, 6.

[227] *Denver Times,* February 28, 1902, 1.

[228] *Denver Times,* February 28, 1902, 1.

[229] *Denver Times,* March 3, 1902, 1.

[230] *Denver Times,* February 28, 1902, 1.

[231] *Denver Times,* March 1, 1902, 1.

[232] *Denver Times,* March 1, 1902, 1.

[233] *Leadville Herald Democrat,* March 2, 1902, 1.

[234] *Leadville Herald Democrat,* March 2, 1902, 1.

[235] *Leadville Herald Democrat,* March 2, 1902, 1.

[236] *Leadville Herald Democrat,* March 2, 1902, 1.

[237] *Leadville Herald Democrat,* March 3, 1902, 1.

[238] *Leadville Herald Democrat,* March 6, 1902, 1.

[239] *Denver Times,* March 3, 1902, 1.

[240] *Denver Republican,* March 1, 1902, 1.

[241] *Leadville Herald Democrat,* March 1, 1902, 1.

[242] *Denver Times,* March 11, 1902, 1.

[243] *Rocky Mountain News,* March 20, 1906, 1 & 8.

[244] *Denver Westerners Roundup,* Vol. XIV, No. 2., February 1958, 3.

[245] *Leadville Herald Democrat,* November 28, 1905, 1.

[246] *Leadville Herald Democrat,* December 8, 1905, 1.

[247] *Rocky Mountain News,* January 18, 1906, 2.

[248] *Rocky Mountain News,* March 14, 1906.

[249] *Rocky Mountain News,* January 23, 1906, 1.

[250] *Rocky Mountain News,* January 24, 1906, 3.

[251] *Rocky Mountain News,* March 17, 1906, 3.

[252] Wolle, 426.

[253] *Rocky Mountain News,* March 14, 1906.

[254] *Rocky Mountain News,* March 16, 1906, 1 & 5.

[255] *Rocky Mountain News,* January 20, 1906, 12.

[256] *Rocky Mountain News,* March 16, 1906, 5.

[257] *Aspen Democrat,* March 22, 1906, 1.

[258] *Daily Rocky Mountain News,* April 1, 1906, 10.

[259] *Leadville Herald Democrat,* March 24, 1906, 1.

[260] *Rocky Mountain News,* March 23, 1906, 1.

[261] *Leadville Herald Democrat,* March 24, 1906, 1.

[262] *Leadville Herald Democrat,* January 24, 1906, 3.

[263] *Leadville Herald Democrat,* March 24, 1906, 1.

[264] *Rocky Mountain News,* March 19, 1906, 3.

[265] *Rocky Mountain News,* March 19, 1906, 3.

[266] *Rocky Mountain News,* March 18, 1906, 1 & 11.

[267] *Rocky Mountain News,* March 21, 1906, 1 & 5.

[268] *Leadville Herald Democrat,* March 20, 1906, 1.

[269] Sloan, 19.

[270] Ingersoll, 145.

[271] Sloan, 19.

[272] Sloan, 21.

[273] *Daily Rocky Mountain News,* April 1, 1906, 10.

[274] *Leadville Herald Democrat,* March 20, 1906, 1.

[275] *Silverton Standard,* April 7, 1906, 1.

[276] *Leadville Herald Democrat,* March 20, 1906, 1.

[277] *Rocky Mountain News,* March 20, 1906, 8.

[278] *Rocky Mountain News,* March 21, 1906, 5.

[279] *Rocky Mountain News,* March 22, 1906, 6.

[280] *Rocky Mountain News,* March 23, 1906, 2.

[281] *Leadville Herald Democrat,* March 19, 1906, 1.

[282] *Leadville Herald Democrat,* March 19, 1906, 1.

[283] Betsy R. Armstrong and Knox Williams, *The Avalanche Book* (Golden: Fulcrum Publishing, 1992): 37.

[284] *Rocky Mountain News,* March 19, 1906, 1 & 3.

[285] *Rocky Mountain News,* March 20, 1906, 1.

[286] *Rocky Mountain News,* March 19, 1906, 3.

[287] *Rocky Mountain News,* March 19, 1906, 3.

[288] Armstrong and Williams, 36.

[289] *Rocky Mountain News,* March 10, 1963, 32.

[290] *Denver Post,* February 18, 1936.

[291] *Rocky Mountain News,* August 23, 1960, 31.

[292] Wolle, 208-209.

[293] Poor, 367.

[294] Josie Moore Crum, *Rails Among the Peaks,* (St. Paul: Railroader Printing House, 1956): 257.

[295] *Randall Clippings,* Vol. 2, P.269, January 1916.

[296] *Rocky Mountain News,* July 13, 1920, 1.

[297] *Carbonate Chronicle,* January 24, 1916, 1.

[298] Dale Gallegher, ed., *The Snowy Torrents, Avalanche Accidents in the United States 1910-1966,* (Alta: USDA, USFS, Avalanche Study Center, 1967): 8-10.

[299] *Leadville Herald Democrat,* January 23, 1962, 3.

[300] John Marshall and Jerry Roberts, *Living (and dying) In Avalanche Country* (Silverton: A Simpler Way Book Co., 1992) 55.

[301] Marshall and Roberts, 55.

[302] *Gunnison News Champion,* March 28, 1929, 1.

[303] *Leadville Herald Democrat,* February 26, 1936, 1.

[304] *Leadville Herald Democrat,* February 27, 1936, 1.

[305] *Leadville Herald Democrat,* February 24, 1936, 1.

[306] *Denver Post,* February 18, 1936.

[307] *Denver Post,* February 18, 1936.

[308] *Denver Post,* February 18, 1936.

[309] *Denver Post,* May 1, 1936.

[310] *Leadville Herald Democrat,* February 18, 1936, 1.

[311] *Denver Post,* February 24, 1936, 1.

[312] *Denver Post,* February 25, 1936, 1.

[313] *Leadville Herald Democrat,* February 26, 1936, 1.

[314] *Rocky Mountain News,* February 25, 1936, 1.

[315] *Leadville Herald Democrat,* February 26, 1936, 1.

316 *Rocky Mountain News,* April 1, 1936, 1.
317 *Rocky Mountain News,* February 25, 1936, 1.
318 *Rocky Mountain News,* September 3, 1941, 1.
319 Marshall and Roberts, 59.
320 *Rocky Mountain News,* January 22, 1962, 2.
321 Gallegher, 73-75.
322 E. D. Fales, Jr., "Terror at Twin Lakes," *Popular Science,* (Vol 182, February 1963): 115.
323 Fales, 115-116.
324 Gallegher, 73.
325 Fales, 116.
326 Nels G. Lindstone, *Herald Democrat,* February 10, 1967, 1.
327 Gallegher, 74.
328 Fales, 117.
329 Barbara Adamich, "Avalanche!," *Contemporary Magazine,* (*Denver Post,* April 15, 1962): 10.
330 Gallegher, 74.
331 Gallegher, 74.
332 Adamich, 10.
333 Adamich, 24.
334 Gallegher, 73.
335 Gallegher, 88.
336 *Rocky Mountain News,* March 10, 1963, 32.
337 Zeke Scher, "Avalanches: Colorado's White Death," *Empire Magazine,* Denver Post, December 1, 1974: 53.
338 Gallegher, 88-91.
339 United States Forest Service. *Snow Avalanches, A Handbook of Forecasting and Control Measures,* FSH2 2332.81. US Department of Agriculture, Washington: USGPO, 1961, 6.
340 *Rocky Mountain News,* February 16, 1989.
341 Scher, 47.
342 Armstrong and Williams, 43.
343 *Denver Post,* April 9, 1957, 1.
344 Scher, 53 ff.
345 *Denver Post,* April 9, 1957, 1.
346 *Rocky Mountain News,* April 9, 1957, 5.
347 *Rocky Mountain News,* April 9, 1957, 5.
348 *Rocky Mountain News,* April 9, 1957, 5.
349 *Denver Post,* April 9, 1957, 1.
350 *Rocky Mountain News,* April 10, 1957, 5.
351 *Denver Post,* April 10, 1957, 21.
352 *Denver Post,* March 17, 1987, 3C.
353 *Denver Post,* January 3, 1988, 15A.
354 *Denver Post,* January 28, 1993.
355 *Denver Post,* March 17, 1987, 3c.
356 *Denver Post,* March 5, 1987, 4b.
357 *Denver Post,* February 17, 1987, 4B.
358 *Denver Post,* February 17, 1987, 4B.
359 *Denver Post,* February 16, 1987, 3B.
360 *Denver Post,* February 19, 1987, 8A.
361 Mary Logan, Manuscript, Breckenridge, CO, 1987.
362 *Denver Post,* February 26, 1987, 4B.

[363] *Denver Post,* February 19, 1987, 1A.
[364] *Denver Post,* February 19, 1987, 1A.
[365] *Denver Post,* February 20, 1987, 17A.
[366] Mary Logan Manuscript, Breckenridge, Colorado,1987.
[367] *Denver Post,* February 20, 1987, 1A.
[368] *Silverton Standard,* March 24, 1906, 1.